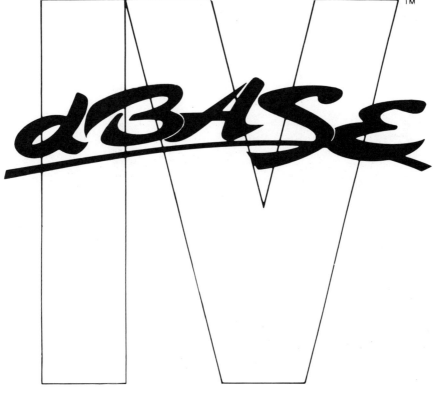

85 dBASE IV™

USER-DEFINED FUNCTIONS AND PROCEDURES

PHILIP STEELE

WINDCREST

Trademarks:

dBASE, dBASE III PLUS, dBASE IV, and *ASHTON-TATE* are trademarks of Ashton-Tate, Inc.

PC DOS is a trademark of IBM Corporation

HP Laserjet is a trademark of Hewlett-Packard Company

Published by **Windcrest Books**

FIRST EDITION/FIRST PRINTING

© 1989 **Windcrest Books**. Reproduction or publication of the content in any manner, without express permission of the publisher, is prohibited. No liability is assumed with respect to the use of the information herein. Printed in the United States of America.

Library of Congress Cataloging-in-Publication Data

Steele, Philip, 1941-
    85 dBASE IV user-defined functions and procedures / by Philip
Steele.
        p. cm.
    Includes index.
    ISBN 0-8306-3236-0 (pbk.)
    1. Data base management. 2. dBASE IV (Computer program)
I. Title. II. Title: Eighty-five dBASE four user-defined functions
and procedures.
QA76.9.D3S735   1989
005.75′65—dc19   88-37338
                                                          CIP

TAB BOOKS Inc. offers software for sale. For information and a catalog, please contact TAB Software Department, Blue Ridge Summit, PA 17294-0850.

Questions regarding the content of this book should be addressed to:

Windcrest Books
Division of TAB BOOKS Inc.
Blue Ridge Summit, PA 17294-0850

Ron Powers: Director of Acquisitions
David M. Harter: Technical Editor
Katherine Brown: Production

Contents

Dedication

To my loving wife Dorothy and daughter Denise who have always encouraged and supported me in all my efforts. I also wish to thank them for providing the time and encouragement necessary to enable me to complete this book.

Acknowledgments

I wish to thank all my friends, colleagues, and clients for their encouragement, ideas and suggestions.

Also I wish to thank ASHTON-TATE for their assistance and for providing me with the dBASE IV software I needed so that I could write this book.

Introduction

This book is not a tutorial for the beginning dBASE IV programmer. It is intended for people who already have written many lines of dBASE code and who wish to improve their code, or to distribute their applications in the corporate marketplace.

This book will not teach you how to program or code in dBASE IV. The purpose of this book is:

- [ ] to explain the User-Defined Functions (UDF) and Procedures as implemented in dBASE IV.
- [ ] to show you when to use dBASE IV User-Defined Functions and Procedures.
- [ ] to show you how to write fast, efficient, errorless dBASE IV User-Defined Functions and Procedures using professional techniques that I have developed in my 25 years as a data processing professional.
- [ ] to provide reference material and practical techniques for both users and developers of dBASE IV systems.

☐ to provide functions that will cover all areas of database programming using User-Defined Functions and be useful in most corporate environments.

Most of these functions have been used to develop commercial applications that have cost tens of thousands of dollars, and are currently being used by some of the largest corporations in the USA.

Setting the Scene

You probably have been using dBASE for a few years now. You know how to add a record to a database; you can change the contents of fields, compute fields and manipulate dates. Now you need to write more-complex applications. You have just obtained dBASE IV and noticed a new feature called the User-Defined Function (UDF), and you want to learn more about it.

This book contains the techniques used by the pros to turn complex hard-to-follow applications into exciting, fast, coherent systems using User-Defined Functions and Procedures. **Note:** These techniques are only for dBASE IV—not dBASE II, dBASE III or dBASE III PLUS.

When nothing else was available, dBASE II and dBASE III PLUS were great. However, with the advent of dBASE IV, there is no good reason to use old releases of dBASE any more, except for some very small non-IBM PC systems.

What Is dBASE IV?

dBASE IV is the latest incarnation of the dBASE language with many new features: an improved user interface, SQL, a pseudo compiler, a good report writer, an excellent screen generator, code writer and User-Defined Functions.

What Is a User-Defined Function?

The User-Defined Function is nothing more than a method to enable dBASE IV programmers to write their own functions using dBASE IV as the source language. It can be used to create functions not provided by dBASE IV, such as changing all proper names to start with an uppercase letter. Why was this functionality provided?

Why Use a User-Defined Function?

Through the use of a User-Defined Function, you the programmer can add any feature you like to dBASE IV. You can: verify data entry fields, add mathematical features that are not present in the language (such as factorials), enhance screen displays, and make your code easier to read and debug.

UDFs and Procedures

User-Defined Functions written in dBASE IV are almost the same as dBASE IV Procedures. You can write as many as you need, compile them, and incorporate them in any or all of your applications. Your applications can use your User-Defined Functions just as if they were native dBASE IV functions, like EOF( ).

In dBASE IV, a User-Defined Function starts with the key-word FUNCTION followed by the function name. A Procedure starts with the key-word PROCEDURE followed by the function name. A User-Defined Function returns a value (any valid dBASE IV data type is permitted); a Procedure does not. A User-Defined Function is called by assigning a variable to it, such as: A = PHIL(X,Y,Z). A Procedure is called using the DO command: DO PHIL WITH X,Y,Z. Sometimes you must write a User-Defined Function as a Procedure because of the dBASE language restrictions. For example, a User-Defined Function may not call a macro. Therefore, if your User-Defined Function needs to set a color, (which is passed to it as a parameter, using the command: "SET COLOR TO &FassedCol"), you must write the User-Defined Function as a Procedure.

A major advantage to User-Defined Functions is that, once they are written and tested, they can be used in any appropriate situation without any additional debugging problems. Thus, a library of useful, tested functions can be written and incorporated into new code without repeating the debugging process.

dBASE IV Environment

The requirements for dBASE IV are, more or less, those for any PC-based application—namely an IBM PC or compatible (an AT class machine, or better, is preferred) with a hard disk, 640K of memory, a color monitor and printer.

If you are developing small systems for your own use, you can get by with a PC, monochrome monitor, and a hard disk. However, the development process might be both painful and slow on that configuration.

How To Use This Book

The following symbols and conventions are used throughout this book. Most are the same as those in dBASE manuals, and others reflect programming styles from other languages and manuals:

SYMBOL	NAME	USE
*	Asterisk	A comment line in dBASE Code.
. . .	Ellipsis	Missing related items or lines of code.
;	Semicolon	Code continued on the next line.
{ }	Braces	Use to show a character that cannot be printed, such as a CHR(27) which is the Escape character and cannot be printed on a LASER printer {Esc}.
[ ]	Brackets	Use to show a variable is needed to replace the generic name placed in the brackets. For example CHECK([Number]) could be written as CHECK(5).
^	Circumflex	Indicates the Control key. ^C would mean press and hold down the control key and then press the "C" key simultaneously.
K	Kilobyte	1,024 bytes.

Versions of the software products used in the code for this book are always being upgraded. The code in this book is written completely in dBASE IV, and has been tested using a beta release of dBASE IV.

1

Data Entry

The most common use of User-Defined Functions is in data entry. In this example, you must make sure the date entered (the hired date) is at least sixteen years later than the previously entered birth date. The UDF is used in conjunction with the VALID clause in a GET statement as follows:

```
@ x1, y1 GET Field1
@ x2, y2 GET Field2
@ x3, y3 GET Field3
@ x4, y4 GET Field4
. . .
@ 12,25 GET HiredDate VALID TestDate (BirthDate)
. . .
READ
```

You can use standard error-checking techniques after performing the read within a DO WHILE loop if you are only checking one or two fields as follows:

```
TestDate = { / / }
* 16 Years = 16 * 365 + 4 = 5844 Days
DO WHILE BirthDate > TestDate - 5844
    @ 12,25 SAY "Enter hire date: " GET HiredDate
    READ
    IF BirthDate > TestDate - 5844
      DO ERR WITH 1
    ENDIF
ENDDO
```

However, if you have a complex screen with many GETs (entry fields), many lines of code are required to test all the entry fields. All corrections are then performed after the last data entry field is filled. Erroneous data will not be corrected at the time of entry, but some time thereafter

If you place a read and error check after each field to avoid this problem, then the user will not be able to go back to a previously entered field and change it.

Both of these problems can be avoided through the use of the User-Defined Function.

The major reason for using User-Defined Functions in data entry is that an automatic branch to the procedure referenced by the VALID condition occurs as soon as the GET field is filled. In the case of the first example, FUNCTION TestDate is executed before any additional GETs are processed. Look at FUNCTION TestDate:

```
FUNCTION TESTDATE
PARAMETERS BirthDate, TestData
IF BirthDate > TestDate - 5844
    DO ERR1
    RETURN (.F.)
ELSE
    RETURN (.T.)
ENDIF
*END:TESTDATE
```

Notice the following attributes associated with this and all User-Defined Functions:

[1] All UDFs start with the FUNCTION statement.
[2] A PARAMETERS statement may be included.
[3] A.T., .F., or value must be returned.
[4] A UDF may call other procedures or functions.
[5] The calling statement will be re-executed until a .T. is returned in a GET. . .READ combination.

Now that you understand what User-Defined Functions are, and how they work, you are almost ready to write your first User-Defined Function.

Each User-Defined Function will be presented in the following form:

[1] A statement of the problem.
[2] A proposed solution using a User-Defined Function.
[3] The code used to invoke the User-Defined Function.
[4] The User-Defined Function itself.
[5] Any comments pursuant to the User-Defined Function.

Now you can finally write your first User-Defined Function.

AGE SCREENING

The problem:

You are entering data about potential employees into your database. Two dates are input: The candidate's birthday, and potential starting date. You must ensure that you do not hire anyone who will be less than 21 years of age when starting work.

The solution:

Use a general-purpose User-Defined Function in conjunction with the GET . . . VALID syntax. This UDF should compare the first date to the second date plus a constant. It will return a .T. if the first date is at least N days less than the second date.

The calling code:

```
*    . . .
     SET COLOR TO &ColStand
     CLEAR
     DEFINE WINDOW Err FROM 22,00 TO 24,79 COLOR W + /R
     STORE { / / } TO Birthday, StartDay
     NDays = 7671          && 21 Years
     @ 10,12 SAY "Birthday: " GET Birthday
     @ 12,10 SAY "Start Date: " GET StartDay;
          VALID DifDate(StartDay, BirthDay, NDays)
     READ
     RELEASE WINDOW Err
*    . . .
```

The User-Defined Function:

```
FUNCTION DIFDATE
*
*   Program...: DIFDATE
*   Author....: Phil Steele - President
*             Phillipps Computer Systems Inc.
*   Address...: 52 Hook Mountain Road,
*             Montville NJ 07045
*   Phone.....: (201) 575-8575
*   Date......: 01/02/89
*   Notice....: Copyright 1989  Philip Steele,
*             All Rights Reserved.
*   Notes.....: This function insures that DATE1 is
*             X days greater than DATE2
*   Parameters: DATE1, DATE2 - Dates to be compared
*             NUMOFDAYS    - The number of days
*                          DATE1 must be greater
*                          than DATE2 for a .T.
*                          result.
*
PARAMETERS Date1, Date2, NumOfDays
PRIVATE    Date1, Date2, NumOfDays
IF Date1 >= Date2 + NumOfDays
   RETURN(.T.)
ELSE
   ACTIVATE WINDOW Err
   @ 0,2 SAY "Start Date must be 21 years later " +;
         "than birthday. - Press space to continue"
   Key = INKEY(5)
   DEACTIVATE WINDOW Err
   RETURN(.F.)
ENDIF
*END:DIFDATE
```

Comments:

Notice that this function is short (this one has only 12 noncomment lines). The condition is checked, an error message is displayed if the condition is not met, and a TRUE or FALSE is returned to the calling code.

VALIDATING JOB TITLES
The problem:

You must assign new employees to a division of the company. Each division has a different set of valid job titles. You must be sure that the entered job title matches one of the valid titles.

The solution:

Use a general-purpose User-Defined Function in conjunction with the GET . . . VALID syntax. This UDF compares the entered division to a passed string of valid job codes that are valid for the division entered.

The calling code

```
*   . . .
SET COLOR TO &ColStand
CLEAR
Job = "      "
ValidJobs = "DRV,HLP,LDR,GUARD,SPVSR,MNGR"
@ 10,12 GET Job VALID MatchStr(Job, ValidJobs)
READ
*   . . .
```

The User-Defined Function:

```
FUNCTION MATCHSTR
*
* Program...: MATCHSTR
* Author....: Phil Steele - President
*             Phillipps Computer Systems Inc.
* Address...: 52 Hook Mountain Road,
*             Montville NJ 07045
* Phone.....: (201) 575-8575
* Date......: 01/02/89
* Notice....: Copyright 1989  Philip Steele,
*             All Rights Reserved.
* Notes.....: This function insures that VAR1 is
*             contained in STR1
* Parameters: VAR1 - The variable to be compared
*             STR1 - A group of string variables
*                    separated by ","
*
PARAMETERS Var1, Str1
PRIVATE    Var1, Str1
Str1 = Str1 + ",,"
DO WHILE .T.
   Comma = AT(",", Str1)
   IF Comma = 0 .OR. LEN(Str1) < 2
      RETURN(.F.)
   ENDIF
   SStr = SUBSTR(Str1, 1, Comma - 1)
   Str1 = SUBSTR(Str1, Comma + 1)
   IF Var1 = SStr
      RETURN(.T.)
   ENDIF
ENDDO
*END:MATCHSTR
```

Comments:

Look at how this UDF works:

[1] Add two commas to the end of the string containing the valid choices to establish an endpoint.
[2] Process until the end of the valid string, or until a match is found.
[3] Find the comma using the AT command.
[4] Check for the end of the valid choices and return FALSE.
[5] Parse Str1 into valid choices.
[6] Return TRUE if Var1 equals the parsed valid choice.

ENTERING BIRTHDAY

The problem:

> You must display the employee's age while entering the employee's birthday in a group of GET statements.

The solution:

> Use a general-purpose User-Defined Function in con-junction with the GET . . . VALID syntax. This UDF checks to see if a valid date is entered, and then display the age while there are still additional GETs pending.

The calling code:

```
*   . . .
SET COLOR TO &Colstand
CLEAR
*   GET . . .
*   GET . . .
BDate = { / / }
@ 10,12 SAY "When were you born: ";
      GET BDate VALID BirthAge (BDate, 12, 3)
*   GET . . .
*   GET . . .
READ
*   . . .
```

The User-Defined Function:

```
FUNCTION BIRTHAGE
*┌─────────────────────────────────────────────────────────┐
*│ Program...: BIRTHAGE                                     │
*│ Author....: Phil Steele - President                     │
*│            Phillipps Computer Systems Inc.              │
*│ Address...: 52 Hook Mountain Road,                      │
*│            Montville NJ 07045                           │
*│ Phone.....: (201) 575-8575                              │
*│ Date......: 01/02/89                                    │
*│ Notice....: Copyright 1989  Philip Steele,             │
*│            All Rights Reserved.                         │
*│ Notes.....: This function checks for a valid date      │
*│            and displays the number of years from       │
*│            the date till today.                         │
*│ Parameters: BDATE   - The date checked for             │
*│                       validity, and used to compute    │
*│                       elapsed years.                    │
*│            X and Y - The coordinates used to           │
*│                       display the elapsed years.        │
*└─────────────────────────────────────────────────────────┘
PARAMETERS BDate, X, Y
PRIVATE    BDate, X, Y
IF MONTH(BDate) < 1
   RETURN(.F.)
ENDIF
EYears = (DATE() - BDate) / 365.25
@ X,Y     SAY "Your age is "
@ X,COL() SAY STR(EYears,2,0)
@ X,COL() SAY " years."
RETURN(.T.)
*END:BIRTHAGE
```

Comments:

User-Defined Functions used with the VALID statement can do more than check validity. This one not only checks validity, but also computes and displays data.

COMPUTING SUMS

The problem:

You must compute the sum of a group of numbers as they are entered so that the subtotal can be checked.

The solution:

Use a general-purpose User-Defined Function in conjunction with the GET . . . VALID syntax. This UDF computes and displays a running subtotal at a specified position on the screen.

The calling code:

```
*   . . .
SET COLOR TO &ColStand
CLEAR
Number   = 1
NewTotal = 0
DO WHILE Number < > 0
   @ 12,12 SAY "Enter Numbers to sum: ";
           GET Number VALID NumSum(Number,22,10);
           PICTURE "9,999.99"
   @ 13,12 SAY "Enter 0 TO stop."
   READ
ENDDO
*   . . .
```

The User-Defined Function:

```
FUNCTION NUMSUM
*
*   Program...: NUMSUM
*   Author....: Phil Steele - President
*             Phillipps Computer Systems Inc.
*   Address...: 52 Hook Mountain Road,
*             Montville NJ 07045
*   Phone.....: (201) 575-8575
*   Date......: 01/02/89
*   Notice....: Copyright 1989  Philip Steele,
*             All Rights Reserved.
*   Notes.....: This function computes a sum of numbers
*             and displays the total while the data
*             is being entered.
*   Parameters: Number  - Entered number.
*             X and Y - The coordinates for the
*                       computed total.
*   Note: NewTotal must be defined in the calling
*         procedure.
*
PARAMETERS Number, X, Y
PRIVATE    Number, X, Y
NewTotal = Number + NewTotal
@ X,Y      SAY "Running Total: "
@ X,COL() SAY NewTotal PICTURE "99,999.99"
RETURN(.T.)
*END:NUMSUM
```

Comments:

This UDF adds the entered number to the variable called NewTotal and displays NewTotal at coordinates X,Y.

SUMMING SEPARATE LINES

The problem:

> A group of numbers are entered on *separate* lines. You must compute their sum so that the subtotal can be viewed and checked.

The solution:

> Use a general-purpose User-Defined Function in conjunction with the GET . . . VALID syntax.

The calling code:

```
*    . . .
    SET COLOR TO &ColStand
    CLEAR
    Public N1, N2, N3, N4, N5, X, Y
    STORE 0 TO N1, N2, N3, N4, N5
    STORE 20 TO X, Y
    @  8,12 SAY "N1: " GET N1 VALID SubTot( );
          PICTURE "9,999.99"
    @ 10,12 SAY "N2: " GET N2 VALID SubTot( );
          PICTURE "9,999.99"
    @ 12,12 SAY "N3: " GET N3 VALID SubTot( );
          PICTURE "9,999.99"
    @ 14,12 SAY "N4: " GET N4 VALID SubTot( );
          PICTURE "9,999.99"
    @ 16,12 SAY "N5: " GET N5 VALID SubTot( );
          PICTURE "9,999.99"
    READ
*    . . .
```

The User-Defined Function:

```
FUNCTION SUBTOT
*
*  Program...: SUBTOT
*  Author....: Phil Steele - President
*             Phillipps Computer Systems Inc.
*  Address...: 52 Hook Mountain Road,
*             Montville NJ 07045
*  Phone.....: (201) 575-8575
*  Date......: 01/02/89
*  Notice....: Copyright 1989  Philip Steele,
*             All Rights Reserved.
*  Notes.....: This function computes a sum of numbers
*             and displays the total while the data
*             is being entered.
*  Parameters: None - However you must declare the
*             numbers to be summed and the row and
*             column values PUBLIC.
*
PRIVATE STotal
STotal = N1 + N2 + N3 + N4 + N5
@ X,Y     SAY "SUBTOTAL:"
@ X,COL() SAY STotal PICTURE "99,999.99"
RETURN(.T.)
*END:SUBTOT
```

Comments:

This UDF differs from NUMSUM in that the subtotal amount will change if the user decides to change a previous entry. Therefore, you must add all the numbers together before displaying the subtotal.

2

Displays

Next to the validation of input data, the most common use of User-Defined Functions is for screen displays. There are many repetitious displays used in one application, or the same code is often used in different applications. Using Procedures or User-Defined Functions in place of repetitious code results in code that is easier to read and maintain.

INTRODUCTORY SCREEN
The problem:

When you start most commercial applications, you are greeted with an introductory screen. Sometimes it is animated, sometimes it is static, but in all cases it tells you what program you are running, and usually the release number. When you write a system, it should look as professional as any of the commercial packages. How will you achieve this goal?

The solution:

Use a general-purpose User-Defined Function to display basic system information for the user on an introductory screen.

The calling code:

```
*    . . .
    SET COLOR TO &ColStand
    CLEAR
    A  =  Intro( )
    A  =  Cent( 9, 80, "Phillipps Computer Systems Inc.")
    A  =  Cent(11, 80, "U.D.F. Demonstration Program")
    A  =   Cent(12, 80, "Release 2.01")
    A  =   Cent(14, 80, "Copyright 1989    Philip Steele")
    SET COLOR TO &ColStand
*    . . .
```

The User-Defined Function:

```
FUNCTION INTRO
*
*    Program...: INTRO
*    Author....: Phil Steele - President
*               Phillipps Computer Systems Inc.
*    Address...: 52 Hook Mountain Road,
*               Montville NJ 07045
*    Phone.....: (201) 575-8575
*    Date......: 01/02/89
*    Notice....: Copyright 1989  Philip Steele,
*               All Rights Reserved.
*    Notes.....: This function presents an exploding
*               box with a drop shadow to be used at
*               the beginning of a system usually to
*               show the system name, author and
*               release number.
*
*               The final Box Values (Top, Left,
*               Bottom, Right) = 7, 20, 16, 60
*    Parameters: None.
*
PRIVATE J, K
SET COLOR TO W+/B,N/W,B,B
CLEAR
SET COLOR TO RG+/R,N/W,B,B
J = 8
DO WHILE J < 12
   K = INT((J-6) * 5)
   SET COLOR TO W+/R
   @ 19-J, 50-K CLEAR TO 5+J, K+30
   @ 19-J, 50-K TO 5+J, K+30 DOUBLE COLOR W+/R
   J = J +.2
ENDDO
SET COLOR TO N/N
@ 21-J,  K+31 CLEAR TO 5+J, K+32
@ 5+J,   52-K CLEAR TO 5+J, K+32
SET COLOR TO RG+/R,N/W,B,B
RETURN(.T.)
*END:INTRO
```

Comments:

To ensure that this is a function rather than a procedure, colors are hard-coded rather than using a macro such as SET COLOR TO "&ColStand". Next, a loop is set up to generate a box where the coordinates are dependent on the loop controlling value. After the final box is drawn, the edges of the drop shadow are drawn and the colors of the display are set to the colors of the inside of the box. Then the function returns to the calling program where the information to be displayed is added.

I could have passed the message I wanted to display, and then had the UDF display the message—it's all a matter of style. In the next Procedure, I pass the message.

A POP-UP SCREEN
The problem:

Now assume that you have an introductory screen with a different problem: data was already on the screen from another part of the application. You need to pop up an introductory screen over the existing data and, after the introductory message is read, return to the existing screen.

The solution:

Use a general-purpose Procedure to display the introductory information, making use of dBASE IV's new window feature which preserves the data beneath it.

The calling code:

```
*    . . .
    SET COLOR TO &ColStand
    CLEAR
    N  =  0                  && Fill the screen.
    DO WHILE N < 25
       Line  =   "Line"  +  CHR(64 + N)  +  " "
       @ N,8 SAY REPLICATE(Line,13)
       N  =  N + 1
    ENDDO
    A1  =  "Phillipps Computer Systems Inc."
    A2  =  "U.D.F. Demonstration Program"
    A3  =  "Release 2.01"
    A4  =  "Copyright 1989     Philip Steele"
    DO Intro1 WITH A1, A2, A3, A4

*    . . .
```

The Procedure:

```
PROCEDURE INTRO1
*
*  Program...: INTRO1
*  Author....: Phil Steele - President
*            Phillipps Computer Systems Inc.
*  Address...: 52 Hook Mountain Road,
*            Montville NJ 07045
*  Phone.....: (201) 575-8575
*  Date......: 01/02/89
*  Notice....: Copyright 1989  Philip Steele,
*            All Rights Reserved.
*  Notes.....: This procedure presents an exploding
*            box using windows to preserves the
*            data beneath. The message displayed
*            shows the system name, author and
*            release number.
*
*            The final Box Values (Top, Left,
*            Bottom, Right) = 7, 20, 16, 60
*  Parameters: A1 - Message line 1.
*            A2 - Message line 2.
*            A3 - Message line 3.
*            A4 - Message line 4.
*
PARAMETERS A1, A2, A3, A4
PRIVATE J, K
CLEAR
CW = "RG+/R,W+/R,W+/R"
DEFINE WINDOW X1  FROM 11,38 TO 13,42 DOUBLE COLOR &CW
DEFINE WINDOW X2  FROM 11,36 TO 13,44 DOUBLE COLOR &CW
DEFINE WINDOW X3  FROM 10,34 TO 13,46 DOUBLE COLOR &CW
DEFINE WINDOW X4  FROM 10,32 TO 13,48 DOUBLE COLOR &CW
DEFINE WINDOW X5  FROM 09,30 TO 14,50 DOUBLE COLOR &CW
DEFINE WINDOW X6  FROM 09,28 TO 14,52 DOUBLE COLOR &CW
DEFINE WINDOW X7  FROM 08,26 TO 15,54 DOUBLE COLOR &CW
DEFINE WINDOW X8  FROM 08,24 TO 15,56 DOUBLE COLOR &CW
DEFINE WINDOW X9  FROM 07,22 TO 16,58 DOUBLE COLOR &CW
DEFINE WINDOW X10 FROM 07,20 TO 16,60 DOUBLE COLOR &CW
ACTIVATE WINDOW X1,X2,X3,X4,X5,X6,X7,X8,X9,X10
@ 1,CentNum(40,A1) SAY A1
@ 2,CentNum(40,A2) SAY A2
@ 5,CentNum(40,A3) SAY A3
@ 6,CentNum(40,A4) SAY A4
Key = INKEY(5)
DEACTIVATE WINDOW  X10,X9,X8,X7,X6,X5,X4,X3,X2,X1
RELEASE    WINDOWS X10,X9,X8,X7,X6,X5,X4,X3,X2,X1
SET COLOR TO &ColStand
*END:INTRO1
```

Comments:

This routine is a procedure, not a function, because windows are used. Ten windows, each slightly larger than the one before it, are defined, activated in order, the messages displayed, and the windows deactivated. By using windows, the data beneath is saved.

ONE-LINE MESSAGE

The problem:

You need to display a one-line message to the user in such a manner that it is noticed.

The solution:

Use a general purpose Procedure to display the one-line message with pizzazz.

The calling code:

```
*   . . .
    SET COLOR TO &ColStand
    CLEAR
    DO Intro2 WITH "P  R  O  C  E  S  S  I  N  G"
*   . . .
```

The Procedure:

```
PROCEDURE INTRO2
*┌──────────────────────────────────────────────────────────┐
*│ Program...: INTRO2                                         │
*│ Author....: Phil Steele - President                        │
*│             Phillipps Computer Systems Inc.                │
*│ Address...: 52 Hook Mountain Road,                         │
*│             Montville NJ 07045                             │
*│ Phone.....: (201) 575-8575                                 │
*│ Date......: 01/02/89                                       │
*│ Notice....: Copyright 1989  Philip Steele,                 │
*│             All Rights Reserved.                           │
*│ Notes.....: This function displays multicolored            │
*│             boxes outlining a center message.              │
*│ Parameters: Message - The message to display or            │
*│                       print.                               │
*└──────────────────────────────────────────────────────────┘
PARAMETERS Message
PRIVATE     Message, A, N
DECLARE C[9]
N = 0
A=CENT(12,80,Message)
DO WHILE N < 8
   C[MOD(N+1,8)+1] = "W+/R"
   C[MOD(N+2,8)+1] = "N/G"
   C[MOD(N+3,8)+1] = "G+/RB"
   C[MOD(N+4,8)+1] = "R+/B"
   C[MOD(N+5,8)+1] = "GR+/BG"
   C[MOD(N+6,8)+1] = "GB+/GR"
   C[MOD(N+7,8)+1] = "BR+/N"
   C[MOD(N+8,8)+1] = "B+/W"
   @   4,0   TO   20,79 DOUBLE COLOR &C[1]
   @   5,3   TO   19,76 DOUBLE COLOR &C[2]
   @   6,6   TO   18,73 DOUBLE COLOR &C[3]
   @   7,9   TO   17,70 DOUBLE COLOR &C[4]
   @   8,12  TO   16,67 DOUBLE COLOR &C[5]
   @   9,15  TO   15,64 DOUBLE COLOR &C[6]
   @  10,18  TO   14,61 DOUBLE COLOR &C[7]
   @  11,21  TO   13,57 DOUBLE COLOR &C[8]
   @  12,22  FILL TO 12,56    COLOR &C[1]
   N = N + 1
ENDDO
RETURN
*END: INTRO2
```

Comments:

This procedure fills an array with eight different colors, and places those eight different colors into concentric boxes on the screen. The message is displayed in the center of the innermost box. The colors of the boxes are changed eight times. This results in a movie marquee effect.

A LOGO
The problem:

When you start most commercial applications, you are greeted with an introductory screen. Sometimes it is animated, sometimes it is static, and sometimes it contains a logo. How can you have a logo appear before the introductory screen?

The solution:

Use a logo User-Defined Function to change commonplace displays into dynamic presentations.

The calling code:

```
*   . . .
    SET COLOR TO &ColStand
    CLEAR
    Speed  =  0
    @ 0,0 GET Speed PICTURE  "999"
    READ
    A  =  LOGO1(Speed)
*   . . .
```

The User-Defined Function:

```
FUNCTION LOGO1
*
*  Program...: LOGO1
*  Author....: Phil Steele - President
*             Phillipps Computer Systems Inc.
*  Address...: 52 Hook Mountain Road,
*             Montville NJ 07045
*  Phone.....: (201) 575-8575
*  Date......: 01/02/89
*  Notice....: Copyright 1989  Philip Steele,
*             All Rights Reserved.
*  Notes.....: This function moves a logo across the
*             screen from left to right stopping at
*             the middle of the screen.
*  Parameters: Speed - A Number used to control the
*                      movement of the display.
*
PARAMETERS Speed
PRIVATE    Speed, N, J, X, Y
Speed = IIF(Speed>=8 .AND. Speed<=10, 11, Speed)
X = SPACE(14)
Y = SPACE(18)
DECLARE LOGO[8]
STORE "███████████████     " TO P1
STORE "████          ████   " TO P2
STORE "  ████        ████   " TO P3
STORE "  ████      ████     " TO P4
STORE "  ████████████       " TO P5
STORE "  ████               " TO P6
STORE "  ████               " TO P7
STORE "████████             " TP P8

STORE "       ████████      " TO C1
STORE "    ████████████     " TO C2
STORE "  ████      █████    " TO C3
STORE "  ████               " TO C4
STORE "  ████               " TO C5
STORE "  ████      █████    " TO C6
STORE "    █████████████    " TO C7
STORE "  ████               " TO C8

STORE "     ██████████      " TO S1
STORE "   █████    ████     " TO S2
STORE "  █████     ██████   " TO S3
STORE "   ██████            " TO S4
STORE "      █████████      " TO S5
STORE " ██        ██████    " TO S6
STORE "  ████     ██████    " TO S7
STORE "   ████████████      " TO S8
```

```
STORE X + P1 + C1 + S1 + Y TO LOGO[1]
STORE X + P2 + C2 + S2 + Y TO LOGO[2]
STORE X + P3 + C3 + S3 + Y TO LOGO[3]
STORE X + P4 + C4 + S4 + Y TO LOGO[4]
STORE X + P5 + C5 + S5 + Y TO LOGO[5]
STORE X + P6 + C6 + S6 + Y TO LOGO[6]
STORE X + P7 + C7 + S7 + Y TO LOGO[7]
STORE X + P8 + C8 + S8 + Y TO LOGO[8]
N = 0
DO WHILE N <= 80
   J = 1
   DO WHILE J <= 8
     @ J+2,0 SAY SUBSTR(LOGO[J], 80 - N) +;
                  REPLICATE(" ", 80 - N)
   J = J + 1
   ENDDO
   N = N + Speed
ENDDO
RETURN(.T.)
*END:LOGO1
```

Comments:

This User-Defined Function saves a representation of the letters ''P C S'' surrounded by spaces in an array of eight elements. These elements are moved across the screen from left to right using a DO loop. The variable ''SPEED'' determines how many characters of the array are moved at one time. A small number (1-3) moves the display slowly across the screen, while a larger number (6-10) moves it quickly. The variable SPEED was implemented as a variable for testing purposes.

Note that the logo is created by using CHR(223) and spaces.

ANOTHER LOGO WITH PIZZAZZ

The problem:

Although the previous logo (LOGO1) is animated, it lacks that certain something. How do you add pizzazz?

The solution:

Use a different logo User-Defined Function to change a dynamic to a scintillating display.

The calling code:

```
*    . . .
    SET COLOR TO &ColStand
    CLEAR
    Speed  =   0
    @ 0,0 GET Speed PICTURE "999"
    READ
    A  =   LOGO2(Speed)
*    . . .
```

The User-Defined Function:

```
FUNCTION LOGO2
*
*   Program...: LOGO2
*   Author....: Phil Steele - President
*             Phillipps Computer Systems Inc.
*   Address...: 52 Hook Mountain Road,
*             Montville NJ 07045
*   Phone.....: (201) 575-8575
*   Date......: 01/02/89
*   Notice....: Copyright 1989  Philip Steele,
*             All Rights Reserved.
*   Notes.....: This function moves a logo across the
*             screen from left to right and right to
*             left stopping at the middle of the
*             screen.
*   Parameters: Speed - A Number used to control the
*                        movement of the display.
*
PARAMETERS Speed
PRIVATE     Speed, N, J, X, Y
X = SPACE(14)
Y = SPACE(18)
DECLARE LOGO[8]
STORE "████████    ████  " TO P1
STORE "███████     ████  " TO P2
STORE "  ███       ███   " TO P3
STORE "  ███       ███   " TO P4
STORE "  ████████        " TO P5
STORE "  ███             " TO P6
STORE "  ████            " TO P7
STORE "█████             " TP P8

STORE "        ████████  " TO C1
STORE "      ██████████  " TO C2
STORE "      ████   ████ " TO C3
STORE "      ███         " TO C4
STORE "      ███         " TO C5
STORE "      ████   ████ " TO C6
STORE "      ████████    " TO C7
STORE "        ██████    " TO C8

STORE "        ████████  " TO S1
STORE "      ████████ ██ " TO S2
STORE "      ████     ██ " TO S3
STORE "      ██████      " TO S4
STORE "         ██████   " TO S5
STORE "      ██     ████ " TO S6
STORE "      █████   ██  " TO S7
STORE "       ████████   " TO S8
STORE X + P1 + C1 + S1 + Y TO LOGO[1]
STORE X + P2 + C2 + S2 + Y TO LOGO[2]
```

```
STORE X + P3 + C3 + S3 + Y TO LOGO[3]
STORE X + P4 + C4 + S4 + Y TO LOGO[4]
STORE X + P5 + C5 + S5 + Y TO LOGO[5]
STORE X + P6 + C6 + S6 + Y TO LOGO[6]
STORE X + P7 + C7 + S7 + Y TO LOGO[7]
STORE X + P8 + C8 + S8 + Y TO LOGO[8]
N = 0
DO WHILE N <= 80
    J = 1
    DO WHILE J <= 8
        IF J = 1 .OR. J = 3 .OR. J = 5 .OR. J = 7
            @ J+2,0 SAY SUBSTR(LOGO[J], 80 - N) +;
                        REPLICATE(" ", 80 - N)
        ELSE
            @ J+2,0 SAY REPLICATE(" ", 80 - N) +;
                        SUBSTR(LOGO[J], 1, N)
        ENDIF
    J = J + 1
    ENDDO
    N = N + Speed
ENDDO
@ 3,0 SAY LOGO[1]
@ 5,0 SAY LOGO[3]
@ 7,0 SAY LOGO[5]
@ 9,0 SAY LOGO[7]
RETURN(.T.)
*END: LOGO2
```

Comments:

This User-Defined Function saves a representation of the letters "P C S" surrounded by spaces in an array of eight elements. These elements are moved across the screen from left to right, and right to left, using two DO loops. The variable "SPEED" determines how many characters of the array are moved at one time. A small number (1-3) moves the display slowly across the screen, and a larger number (6-10) moves it quickly. The variable SPEED was implemented as a variable for testing purposes.

Note that the logo is created by using CHR(223) and spaces.

EXPANDING TITLES

The problem:

On occasion, you need to display a word such as PRO-CESSING in the format P R O C E S S I N G or even P R O C E S S I N G.

The solution:

Use a User-Defined Function to expand a title to include blanks.

The calling code:

```
*    . . .
     SET COLOR TO &ColStand
     CLEAR
     X  =   "PHIL STEELE"
     ? X
     X  =   Title(X)
     ? X
     X  =   Title(X)
     ? X
*    . . .
```

The User-Defined Function:

```
FUNCTION TITLE
*
* ┌──────────────────────────────────────────────────────┐
* │ Program...: TITLE                                      │
* │ Author....: Phil Steele - President                    │
* │             Phillipps Computer Systems Inc.            │
* │ Address...: 52 Hook Mountain Road,                     │
* │             Montville NJ 07045                         │
* │ Phone.....: (201) 575-8575                             │
* │ Date......: 01/02/89                                   │
* │ Notice....: Copyright 1989  Philip Steele,             │
* │             All Rights Reserved.                       │
* │ Notes.....: This procedure inserts blanks after        │
* │             each character in a string.                │
* │ Example...: STRING becomes S T R I N G.                │
* │ Parameters: Express - The expression to convert.       │
* └──────────────────────────────────────────────────────┘
PARAMETERS Express
PRIVATE TLen, N
TLen = LEN(Express)
N    = 1
NewTitle = " "
DO WHILE N <= TLen
   NewTitle = NewTitle + SUBSTR(Express,N,1) + " "
   N = N + 1
ENDDO
RETURN(LTRIM(NewTitle))
*END:TITLE
```

Comments:

This User-Defined Function inserts a blank between each character of the passed variable (Express) by using a substring inside of a DO loop. It could also be written using the STUFF function.

CENTERING MESSAGES

The problem:

At times you need to center a message on the screen, in a report, or in a window. Why should you always have to compute where to start?

The solution:

Develop a User-Defined Function that centers messages based upon their length and the length of the output area.

The calling code:

```
*    . . .
     SET COLOR TO &ColStand
     CLEAR
     Message    =   "This is the message to center"
     @ 12, 0 SAY MessCent(Message, 80)
     @ 14, 45 SAY MessCent(Message, 30)
*    . . .
```

The User-Defined Function:

```
FUNCTION MESSCENT
*┌──────────────────────────────────────────────────────┐
*│  Program...: MESSCENT                                  │
*│  Author....: Phil Steele - President                   │
*│             Phillipps Computer Systems Inc.            │
*│  Address...: 52 Hook Mountain Road,                    │
*│             Montville NJ 07045                         │
*│  Phone.....: (201) 575-8575                            │
*│  Date......: 01/02/89                                  │
*│  Notice....: Copyright 1989  Philip Steele,            │
*│             All Rights Reserved.                       │
*│  Notes.....: This function returns a centered          │
*│             message.                                   │
*│  Parameters: Mess   - The message to center.           │
*│             MaxLen - The maximum length of the         │
*│                       message.                         │
*└──────────────────────────────────────────────────────┘
PARAMETER Mess, MaxLen
PRIVATE    Mess, MaxLen
Mess = LTRIM(TRIM(Mess))
RETURN (REPLICATE(" ", (MaxLen-LEN(Mess))/2) + Mess)
*END:MESSCENT
```

Comments:

This User-Defined Function subtracts the length of the
message from the length of the output area, divides the
result by two, and pads the beginning of the message
with those spaces.

MESSAGE CENTERING WITHOUT SPACES

The problem:

The addition of spaces in front of a message to achieve centering does not always look right when a color display is used. Can you center a message using an alternate method?

The solution:

Develop a different User-Defined Function that centers messages based upon their length, and the length of the output area, without adding spaces.

The calling code:

```
*   . . .
    SET COLOR TO &ColStand
    CLEAR
    A  =  Cent( 9, 80, "Phillipps Computer Systems Inc.")
    A  =  Cent(11, 80, "U.D.F. Demonstration Program")
    A  =  Cent(12, 80, "Release 2.01")
    A  =  Cent(14, 80, "Copyright 1989 Philip Steele")
*   . . .
```

FUNCTION CENT

```
*┌──────────────────────────────────────────────────────────┐
* │ Program...: CENT                                         │
* │ Author....: Phil Steele - President                      │
* │             Phillipps Computer Systems Inc.              │
* │ Address...: 52 Hook Mountain Road,                       │
* │             Montville NJ 07045                           │
* │ Phone.....: (201) 575-8575                               │
* │ Date......: 01/02/89                                     │
* │ Notice....: Copyright 1989  Philip Steele,               │
* │             All Rights Reserved.                         │
* │ Notes.....: This function centers a message based        │
* │             upon the maximum length desired and          │
* │             displays or prints the message at the        │
* │             specified row.                               │
* │ Parameters: XRow    - The row the message will be        │
* │                       displayed upon.                    │
* │             MaxLen  - The length to use to compute       │
* │                       the center of the message.         │
* │             Message - The message to display or          │
* │                       print.                             │
* └──────────────────────────────────────────────────────────┘
PARAMETERS XRow, MaxLen, Message
PRIVATE XRow, XCol, MaxLen, Message
XCol = (MaxLen - LEN(Message)) / 2
@ XRow, XCol SAY Message
RETURN (.T.)
*END:CENT
```

Comments:

This User-Defined Function subtracts the length of the message from the length of the output area, divides the result by two, and prints the message at the passed row and computed column.

MESSAGE IN A WINDOW
The problem:

You have placed a window on the screen, and you wish to display a message centered in this window. However the width of the window is variable. What are you going to do?

The solution:

Develop a different User-Defined Function that centers messages based upon the width of a window.

The calling code:

```
*    . . .
     SET COLOR TO &ColStand
     CLEAR
     A1  =   "Phillipps Computer Systems Inc."
     A2  =   "U.D.F. Demonstration Program"
     X1  =   5
     X2  =   45
     X3  =   31
     X4  =   79
     DEFINE WINDOW X1 FROM 3,X1 TO 8,X2 DOUBLE
     DEFINE WINDOW X2 FROM 13,X3 TO 18,X4
     ACTIVATE WINDOW X1
     @ 1,CentNum(X2-X1,A1) SAY A1
     @ 2,CentNum(X2-X1,A2) SAY A2
     ACTIVATE WINDOW X2
     @ 1,CentNum(X4-X3,A1) SAY A1
     @ 2,CentNum(X4-X3,A2) SAY A2
*    . . .
```

The User-Defined Function:

```
FUNCTION CENTNUM
*┌──────────────────────────────────────────────────────┐
*│  Program...: CENTNUM                                   │
*│  Author....: Phil Steele - President                   │
*│              Phillipps Computer Systems Inc.           │
*│  Address...: 52 Hook Mountain Road,                    │
*│              Montville NJ 07045                        │
*│  Phone.....: (201) 575-8575                            │
*│  Date......: 01/02/89                                  │
*│  Notice....: Copyright 1989  Philip Steele,            │
*│              All Rights Reserved.                      │
*│  Notes.....: This function returns the column          │
*│              number used to center a message.          │
*│  Parameters: MaxLen  - The length to use to compute    │
*│                        the center of the message.      │
*│              Message - The message to center.          │
*└──────────────────────────────────────────────────────┘
PARAMETERS MaxLen, Message
PRIVATE    MaxLen, Message
RETURN((MaxLen - LEN(Message)) / 2)
*END:CENTNUM
```

Comments:

This User-Defined Function subtracts the length of the message from the length of the output area, divides the result by two, and returns this value to the calling procedure.

EASY WINDOWING

The problem:

> You are always opening up windows on the screen in different forms, with and without drop shadows, with different colors and different borders. How can you reduce the number of lines of code you must write, and make the application easier to read and debug at the same time?

The solution:

> Develop a Procedure that creates these various boxes.

The calling code:

```
*    . . .
     SET COLOR TO &ColStand
     CLEAR
     WName     =    "TempWin"
     BoxColor  =    "W + /RB,RG + /N,B"
     DO Box WITH WName,7,19,14,60,"D",.T.,"&BoxColor"
     @ 1,1 SAY "Window 0"
     WName1    =    "TempWin1"
     BoxColor  =    "W + /G,N/G,B"
     DO Box WITH WName1,2,2,11,13,"S",.T.,"&BoxColor"
     @ 1,1 SAY "Window 1"
     WName2    =    "TempWin2"
     BoxColor  =    "RG + /R,W + /N,B"
     DO Box WITH WName2,17,59,22,76,"N",.T.,"&BoxColor"
     @ 1,1 SAY "Window 2"
     WName3    =    "TempWin3"
     BoxColor  =    "N/RG,W + /B,B"
     DO Box WITH WName3,18,2,22,22,"D",.F.,"&BoxColor"
     @ 1,1 SAY "Window 3"
     WName4    =    "TempWin4"
     BoxColor  =    "N/W,N/R,B"
     DO Box WITH WName4,0,62,7,78,"N",.F.,"&BoxColor"
     @ 1,1 SAY "Window 4"
     Key = INKEY(0)
     DEACTIVATE  WINDOW
     &WName,&WName1,&WName2,&WName3,;
     &WName4,STempWin,STempWin1,STempWin2
     RELEASE     WINDOW
     &WName,&WName1,&WName2,&WName3,;
     &WName4,STempWin,STempWin1,STempWin2
*    . . .
```

The Procedure:

```
PROCEDURE BOX
*
*┌────────────────────────────────────────────────────┐
*│ Program...: BOX                                      │
*│ Author....: Phil Steele - President                 │
*│             Phillipps Computer Systems Inc.          │
*│ Address...: 52 Hook Mountain Road,                   │
*│             Montville NJ 07045                        │
*│ Phone.....: (201) 575-8575                           │
*│ Date......: 01/02/89                                  │
*│ Notice....: Copyright 1989  Philip Steele,           │
*│             All Rights Reserved.                     │
*│ Notes.....: This function returns a window with      │
*│             optional drop shadow and no, single,     │
*│             or double border.                        │
*│ Parameters: WName  - The name of the window.         │
*│ Parameters: T      - The top of the window.          │
*│             L      - The left of the window.         │
*│             B      - The bottom of the window.       │
*│             R      - The right of the window.        │
*│             SD     - Draw a single "S", double "D"   │
*│                      or "N" border.                  │
*│             Shadow - Should a shadow be drawn?       │
*│             BColor - Color of the box.               │
*└────────────────────────────────────────────────────┘
*
PARAMETERS WName,T, L, B, R, SD, Shadow, BColor
DEFINE WINDOW &WName FROM T,L TO B,R NONE COLOR &BColor
BB = B - T
BR = R - L
IF Shadow
   SName = "S" + WName
   DEFINE WINDOW &SName FROM T+1,L+1 TO B+1,R+2;
             NONE COLOR N,N,N
   ACTIVATE WINDOW &SName
ENDIF
ACTIVATE WINDOW &WName
DO CASE
   CASE SD = "D"
      Kind = "DOUBLE"
   CASE SD = "S"
      Kind = " "
   CASE SD = "N"
      Kind = "NONE"
ENDCASE
SET COLOR TO &BColor
@ 0,0 TO BB,BR &Kind
RETURN
*END:BOX
```

Comments:

This Procedure defines a window without a border using the passed corners (T, L, B, R) and the passed color (&BColor). If necessary, it computes and draws a drop shadow window (windows are used to save the underlying data). Both windows are activated (the drop shadow window first), the requested color is set, and border type drawn before returning to the calling code.

EASY MENUING

The problem:

> You are always using menus surrounded by different boxes, with and without drop shadows, with different colors and different borders. How can you reduce the number of lines of code you write, and make the application easier to read and debug at the same time?

The solution:

> Develop a Procedure that creates these different boxes for use with menus.

The calling code:

```
*    . . .
     SET COLOR TO &ColStand
     CLEAR
     SET COLOR TO &ColMenu
     DO NOWINBOX WITH 10,32,14,48,"D",.T.,"&ColMenu"
     DEFINE MENU Test
     DEFINE PAD A OF Test PROMPT "1. Add Date. " AT 11,33
     DEFINE PAD B OF Test PROMPT "2. View Data." AT 12,33
     DEFINE PAD C OF Test PROMPT "3. Return    " AT 13,33
     ON SELECTION PAD A OF Test DO TCode WITH 1
     ON SELECTION PAD B OF Test DO TCode WITH 2
     ON SELECTION PAD C OF Test DO TCode WITH 3
     ACTIVATE MENU Test
*    . . .
*───────────────────
PROCEDURE TCODE
*───────────────────
PARAMETERS Choice
DO CASE
  CASE Choice  =   1
    @ 22,34 SAY " Add Chosen."
  CASE Choice  =   2
    @ 22,34 SAY "View Chosen."
  CASE Choice  =   3
    DEACTIVATE MENU
    RELEASE    MENU
    SET COLOR TO &ColStand
    RETURN TO MASTER
ENDCASE
RETURN
*END:TCODE
```

The Procedure:

```
PROCEDURE NOWINBOX
*┌────────────────────────────────────────────────────────┐
*│ Program...: NOWINBOX                                     │
*│ Author....: Phil Steele - President                      │
*│            Phillipps Computer Systems Inc.               │
*│ Address...: 52 Hook Mountain Road,                       │
*│            Montville NJ 07045                            │
*│ Phone.....: (201) 575-8575                               │
*│ Date......: 01/02/89                                     │
*│ Notice....: Copyright 1989  Philip Steele,               │
*│            All Rights Reserved.                          │
*│ Notes.....: This function returns a box with an          │
*│            optional drop shadow and no, single,          │
*│            or double border.                             │
*│ Parameters: T      - The top of the box.                 │
*│            L      - The left of the box.                 │
*│            B      - The bottom of the box.               │
*│            R      - The right of the box.                │
*│            SD     - Draw a single "S", double "D"        │
*│                     or "N" border.                       │
*│            Shadow - Should a shadow be drawn?            │
*│            BColor - Color of the box.                    │
*└────────────────────────────────────────────────────────┘
PARAMETERS T, L, B, R, SD, Shadow, BColor
BB = B - T
BR = R - L
IF Shadow
   SET COLOR TO N/N
   @ T+1,L+1 CLEAR TO B+1,R+2
ENDIF
SET COLOR TO &BColor
DO CASE
   CASE SD = "D"
      Kind = "DOUBLE"
   CASE SD = "S"
      Kind = " "
   CASE SD = "N"
      Kind = "NONE"
ENDCASE
@ T,L CLEAR TO B,R
@ T,L       TO B,R &Kind
RETURN
*END:NOWINBOX
```

Comments:

This Procedure draws a drop shadow (if requested) and a box with the proper border using the passed corners (T, L, B, R), and the passed color (&BColor), before returning to the calling code.

The calling procedure is a simple example showing the use of the new dBASE IV menu syntax.

YES OR NO PROMPT
The problem:

How many times do you ask the user if they want to proceed with or cancel the current application? For example: "Do you wish to print the report? (Yes or No):"

The solution:

Develop a Procedure that you can call from anywhere in the system to ask yes or no questions.

The calling code:

```
*    . . .
    SET COLOR TO &ColStand
    CLEAR
    Mess1  =   "DO YOU WISH TO"
    Mess2  =   " DELETE THIS RECORD?"
    YN     =  .F.
    SET COLOR TO &ColStand
    CLEAR
    DO YesOrNo WITH Mess1, Mess2, "&ColError", YN
    ? YN
*    . . .
```

```
PROCEDURE YESORNO
*
*┌─────────────────────────────────────────────────────┐
*│ Program...: YESORNO                                   │
*│ Author....: Phil Steele - President                   │
*│             Phillipps Computer Systems Inc.           │
*│ Address...: 52 Hook Mountain Road,                    │
*│             Montville NJ 07045                        │
*│ Phone.....: (201) 575-8575                            │
*│ Date......: 01/02/89                                  │
*│ Notice....: Copyright 1989  Philip Steele,            │
*│             All Rights Reserved.                      │
*│ Notes.....: This function displays a box containing   │
*│             a question. A user can choose either a    │
*│             Y or N response. The Y or N is then       │
*│             returned by the procedure.                │
*│ Parameters: Mess1    - The first message line to      │
*│                        be displayed.                  │
*│             Mess2    - The second message line to     │
*│                        be displayed.                  │
*│             BoxColor - The color for the displayed    │
*│                        box.                           │
*└─────────────────────────────────────────────────────┘
PARAMETERS Mess1, Mess2, BoxColor, YN
PRIVATE Special, B1, B2, B3
Special = '"-","=","│","║","┌","┐","└","┘"'
*
*    ┌──┐
*    └──┘
B2 = 0
B3 = 20
B1 = LEN(Mess1)
B2 = (40-B1)/2
IF .NOT. EMPTY(Mess2)
   B1 = LEN(Mess2)
   B3 = (40-B1)/2
ENDIF
WName = "Temp"
DO Box WITH WName,7,19,15,62,"D",.T.,"&BoxColor"
@  1,B2 SAY Mess1
@  2,B3 SAY Mess2
@ 4,8  TO 6,14 &Special
@ 4,28 TO 6,34 &Special
DEFINE MENU YNMenu
DEFINE PAD Yes OF YNMenu PROMPT "Yes" AT 5,9
DEFINE PAD No  OF YNMenu PROMPT " No" AT 5,29
ON SELECTION PAD Yes OF YNMenu DO MAKEYN WITH YN, WName
ON SELECTION PAD No  OF YNMenu DO MAKEYN WITH YN, WName
ACTIVATE MENU YNMenu PAD No
RETURN
*END:YESORNO
```

```
PROCEDURE MAKEYN
PARAMETERS YN, WName
YN = IIF(PAD()="YES", .T., .F.)
DEACTIVATE MENU
RELEASE    MENU
DEACTIVATE WINDOW &WName
RELEASE    WINDOW &WName
RETURN
*END:MAKEYN
```

Comments:

This Procedure uses a horizontal menu, in the requested color, to ask the passed question which can be answered by Yes or No. After the user selects Yes or No, the last passed parameter is set to true for yes, or false for no. The original screen is restored before returning to the calling code.

MESSAGE BORDER COLOR

The problem:

Many times it is necessary to change the color of the border around a message, or even make it blink, without affecting the color of the message inside of the border.

The solution:

Develop a Procedure that changes the border color around a message without changing the color of the message.

The calling code:

```
*    . . .
SET COLOR TO &ColStand
CLEAR
X  =  "THIS IS A TEST"
@ 2,2 CLEAR TO 22,70
@ 2,2     TO 22,70 DOUBLE
@ 12,12 SAY X
@ 14,12 SAY "Press any key to continue."
Key  =  INKEY(0)
DO BoxColor WITH 2,2,22,70,"RG + /R","D"
@ 14,12 SAY X
@ 14,12 SAY "Press any key to continue."
Key  =  INKEY(0)
*    . . .
```

The Procedure:

```
PROCEDURE BOXCOLOR
*┌──────────────────────────────────────────────────────────────┐
*│  Program...: BOXCOLOR                                          │
*│  Author....: Phil Steele - President                          │
*│              Phillipps Computer Systems Inc.                  │
*│  Address...: 52 Hook Mountain Road,                           │
*│              Montville NJ 07045                               │
*│  Phone.....: (201) 575-8575                                   │
*│  Date......: 01/02/89                                         │
*│  Notice....: Copyright 1989  Philip Steele,                   │
*│              All Rights Reserved.                             │
*│  Notes.....: This function changes the color of a            │
*│              single or double line box around a              │
*│              message without changing the color of          │
*│              the message.                                     │
*│  Parameters: T  - The top row of the box.                    │
*│              L  - The top column of the box.                 │
*│              B  - The bottom row of the box.                 │
*│              R  - The bottom column of the box.              │
*│              C  - The new color for the box.                 │
*│              SD - "S" = a single box and                     │
*│                   "D" = a double box.                        │
*└──────────────────────────────────────────────────────────────┘
PARAMETERS T,L,B,R,C,SD
PRIVATE    T,L,B,R,C,SD,OldC
IF SD = "D"
   @ T,L TO B,R DOUBLE COLOR &C
ELSE
   @ T,L TO B,R COLOR &C
ENDIF
RETURN
*END:BOXCOLOR
```

Comments:

This Procedure draws a new box of the requested type
(single or double) and color, and then returns to the
calling code.

MESSAGE COLOR

The problem:

At times I found it necessary to change the color of a message, or even make it blink, without affecting the other colors in the system.

The solution:

Develop a Procedure that changes the color of a message without changing the rest of the colors in the system.

The calling code:

```
*    . . .
SET COLOR TO &ColStand
CLEAR
X  =  "THIS IS A TEST"
@ 2,2 CLEAR TO 22,70
@ 2,2      TO 22,70 DOUBLE
@ 16,12 SAY X
@ 18,12 SAY "Press any key to continue."
Key  =  INKEY(0)
DO MessCol WITH 16,12,X,"RG + */BR"
@ 16,12 SAY X
@ 18,12 SAY "Press any key to continue."
Key  =   INKEY(0)
*    . . .
```

The Procedure:

```
PROCEDURE MESSCOL
*
* | Program...: MESSCOL
* | Author....: Phil Steele - President
* |             Phillipps Computer Systems Inc.
* | Address...: 52 Hook Mountain Road,
* |             Montville NJ 07045
* | Phone.....: (201) 575-8575
* | Date......: 01/02/89
* | Notice....: Copyright 1989  Philip Steele,
* |             All Rights Reserved.
* | Notes.....: This function changes the color of a
* |             message without affecting any other
* |             colors.
* | Parameters: R  - The row the message starts on.
* |             C  - The column the message starts on.
* |             M  - The message.
* |             NC - The new color for the message.
*
PARAMETERS R, C, M, NC
PRIVATE    R, C, M, NC
SET COLOR TO &NC
@ R,C SAY M
RETURN
*END:MESSCOL
```

Comments:

This Procedure rewrites the message in the specified color, at the specified row and column, and returns to the calling code.

PSEUDO-NUMERIC DATA

The problem:

You need to display two pseudo-numeric fields so that the output looks like 999/999. A pseudo-numeric field is defined as character data, but only contains numeric data. This type of field is used when there is no need to involve the field in arithmetic operations. A problem appears when the data is not justified in the field, and the screen displays 3 / 9 instead of 3/9.

The solution:

Use a general-purpose User-Defined Function to justify pseudo-numeric data.

The calling code:

```
*    . . .
     SET COLOR TO &ColStand
     CLEAR
     X  =  " 1 "
     Y  =  " 22"
     @ 12,12 SAY X PICTURE "!!!"
     @ 12,15 SAY "/"
     @ 12,16 SAY Y PICTURE "!!!"
     @ 14,12 SAY NTRIM(X,3) PICTURE "!!!"
     @ 14,15 SAY "/"
     @ 14,16 SAY LTRIM(Y) PICTURE "!!!"
*    . . .
```

The User-Defined Function:

```
FUNCTION NTRIM
*┌─────────────────────────────────────────────────────────────┐
*│ Program...: NTRIM                                           │
*│ Author....: Phil Steele - President                        │
*│             Phillipps Computer Systems Inc.                │
*│ Address...: 52 Hook Mountain Road,                         │
*│             Montville NJ 07045                             │
*│ Phone.....: (201) 575-8575                                 │
*│ Date......: 01/02/89                                       │
*│ Notice....: Copyright 1989  Philip Steele,                 │
*│             All Rights Reserved.                           │
*│ Notes.....: This function returns a right                  │
*│             justified pseudo-numeric field                 │
*│ Parameters: PNum - The pseudo-numeric variable            │
*│             PLen - The field length.                       │
*└─────────────────────────────────────────────────────────────┘
PARAMETERS PNum, PLen
RETURN(STR(VAL(PNum),PLen,0))
*END:NTRIM
```

Comments:

This UDF converts the character string to a number
(VAL(PNum)), and then converts this number back to
a string of length PLen which always right-justifies the
pseudo-number the correct number of places.

FIELD WITH LEADING ZEROS

The problem:

You need to display two numeric fields with leading zeros so that the output looks like 0009/0098.

The solution:

Use a general-purpose User-Defined Function to zero-fill the display of a numeric field.

The calling code:

```
*   . . .
SET COLOR TO &ColStand
CLEAR
X  =  1
Y  =  22
@ 12,12 SAY X PICTURE "9999"
@ 12,16 SAY "/"
@ 12,17 SAY Y PICTURE "9999"
SX  =  ZFILL(X,4)
SY  =  ZFILL(Y,4)
@ 14,12 SAY SX PICTURE "!!!!"
@ 14,16 SAY "/"
@ 14,17 SAY SY PICTURE "!!!!"
*   . . .
```

The User-Defined Function:

```
FUNCTION ZFILL
*
*  Program...: ZFILL
*  Author....: Phil Steele - President
*             Phillipps Computer Systems Inc.
*  Address...: 52 Hook Mountain Road,
*             Montville NJ 07045
*  Phone.....: (201) 575-8575
*  Date......: 01/02/89
*  Notice....: Copyright 1989  Philip Steele,
*             All Rights Reserved.
*  Notes.....: This function display a numeric field
*             justified with leading zeros.
*  Parameters: Num  - The numeric field.
*             Size - The total field length.
*
PARAMETERS Num, Size
PRIVATE NewNum, N
NewNum = LTRIM(STR(Num,19,0))
N      = LEN(NewNum)
NewNum = REPLICATE("0", Size - N) + NewNum
RETURN(NewNum)
*END:ZFILL
```

Comments:

This UDF converts the number to a character string of
length 19 (the maximum length of a number). It then
computes how many zeros are needed, based upon the
passed parameter (Size) and the length of the field. It
then returns a character string to the calling procedure.

INSERTING COMMENTS

The problem:

You need to insert comments into a database from any input screen in the system using a pop-up window. If the comment window hides needed data, the user must be able to move the window out of the way. However, the window cannot move to restricted areas of the screen.

The solution:

Use a Procedure to create this moving data entry pop-up window.

The calling code:

```
*    . . .
     SET COLOR TO &ColWarning
     CLEAR
     @ 0, 0 TO 24, 79 DOUBLE
     SET COLOR TO &ColStand
     @ 2, 6 TO 22, 70
     N  =  4        && Fill the screen.
     DO WHILE N < 21
        Line  =  "Line" + CHR(64 + N) + " "
        @ N,8 SAY REPLICATE(Line,10)
        N  =  N + 1
ENDDO
     mCom1  =  "This is the 1st comment. "
     mCom2  =  "This is the 2nd comment. "
     mCom3  =  "This is the 3rd comment. "
     mCom4  =  "This is the 4th comment. "
     mCom5  =  "This is the 5th comment. "
     @ 22,14 SAY "Press F10 to Pop-up Comments –" + ;
                 "Any other key to exit"
     Key = INKEY(0)
     IF Key <> 10Key
        RETURN
     ENDIF
     @ 22,9 SAY "The arrow keys (" + CHR(27) + ;
        CHR(26) + CHR(24) + CHR(25) + ") move ";
        + "the boxes – A/Z change comments."
     TT  =  7
     LL  =  30
     BB  =  13
     RR  =  58
     WinColor  =  "RG + /R,N/W,W + /R"
     DO MOVEWIN WITH TT,LL,BB,RR,2,22,6,70,WinColor
*    . . .
```

The Procedure

```
PROCEDURE MOVEWIN
*
*┌─────────────────────────────────────────────────────────┐
*│ Program...: MOVEWIN                                      │
*│ Author....: Phil Steele - President                     │
*│            Phillipps Computer Systems Inc.              │
*│ Address...: 52 Hook Mountain Road,                      │
*│            Montville NJ 07045                           │
*│ Phone.....: (201) 575-8575                              │
*│ Date......: 01/02/89                                    │
*│ Notice....: Copyright 1989  Philip Steele,             │
*│            All Rights Reserved.                        │
*│ Notes.....: This function pops-up a window on the      │
*│            screen and through the use of various       │
*│            function keys permits you to move the       │
*│            window to other parts of the screen.        │
*│            In addition you can change the values       │
*│            appearing in the window.                    │
*│ Parameters: T     - Top row of pop-up box.             │
*│            L     - Top column of pop-up box.           │
*│            B     - Bottom row of pop-up box.           │
*│            R     - Bottom column of pop-up box.        │
*│            TLimit - Top limit on movement.             │
*│            BLimit - Bottom limit on movement.          │
*│            LLimit - Left limit on movement.            │
*│            RLimit - Right limit on movement.           │
*│            WC    - The color of the window.            │
*└─────────────────────────────────────────────────────────┘
PARAMETERS T,L,B,R,TLimit,BLimit,LLimit,RLimit,WC
PRIVATE     T,L,B,R,MoveKey,TL,BL,LL,RL,WC
SET COLOR TO &WC
DEFINE WINDOW Comment FROM T,L TO B,R DOUBLE COLOR &WC
ACTIVATE WINDOW Comment
TL = TLimit + 1
BL = BLimit - 1
LL = LLimit + 1
RL = RLimit - 1
@ 0,1 SAY mCom1
@ 1,1 SAY mCom2
@ 2,1 SAY mCom3
@ 3,1 SAY mCom4
@ 4,1 SAY mCom5
MoveKey = 0
DO WHILE MoveKey <> Escape
   MoveKey = INKEY(0)
   DO CASE
      CASE MoveKey = CurUp .AND. T > TL
         T = T - 1
         B = B - 1
      CASE MoveKey = CurDn .AND. B < BL
         T = T + 1
         B = B + 1
```

```
            CASE MoveKey = CurLeft .AND. L > LL
                L = L - 1
                R = R - 1
            CASE MoveKey = CurRight .AND. R < RL
                L = L + 1
                R = R + 1
            CASE MoveKey >= ASC(" ") .AND. ;
                 MoveKey <= ASC("z")
                SET COLOR TO &ColEntry
                mCom1 = CHR(LASTKEY()) + SUBSTR(mCom1,2)
                @ 0,1 GET mCom1
                @ 1,1 GET mCom2
                @ 2,1 GET mCom3
                @ 3,1 GET mCom4
                @ 4,1 GET mCom5
                READ
                SET COLOR TO &ColMenu
                SET CONFIRM ON
                EXIT
        ENDCASE
        MOVE WINDOW Comment TO T, L
    ENDDO
DEACTIVATE WINDOW Comment
RETURN
*END:MOVEWIN
```

Comments:

This Procedure defines and activates the data entry
window using the passed parameters (T, L, B, R and WC
for color). The movement limits are established, and
INKEY(0) is called awaiting input. A CASE structure is
created to act on the entered key stroke. The window
is moved if a cursor key (up, down, left, or right arrow)
is pressed. The movement of the window is restricted
to the active screen area as defined by the user. If a letter,
number, or key between " " CHR(32) and "z" CHR(122)
is pressed, it is saved and used as the first keystroke for
data entry. After data entry is completed the window
is deactivated and control is returned to the calling code.

DOLLAR FORMAT

The problem:

At times you might find it necessary to display a number as a dollar amount—similar to the RANGE FORMAT DOLLARS command of a spreadsheet package.

The solution:

Develop a User-Defined Function that displays a number as a dollar amount.

The calling code:

```
*    . . .
SET COLOR TO &ColStand
CLEAR
X  =  123456.7
Y  =  Dollars(X)
?Y
X  =  - 23456.7
Y  =  Dollars(X)
? Y
*    . . .
```

The User-Defined Function:

```
FUNCTION DOLLARS
*
*| Program...: DOLLARS
*| Author....: Phil Steele - President
*|             Phillipps Computer Systems Inc.
*| Address...: 52 Hook Mountain Road,
*|             Montville NJ 07045
*| Phone.....: (201) 575-8575
*| Date......: 01/02/89
*| Notice....: Copyright 1989  Philip Steele,
*|             All Rights Reserved.
*| Notes.....: This function displays a number as a
*|             dollar amount.
*| Parameters: X  - The number to display as a dollar
*|                  amount.
*
PARAMETERS X
PRIVATE Z
Z = LTRIM(TRANSFORM(X, "999,999,999,999.99"))
Z = IIF(X>0, "$"+Z, "-$"+SUBSTR(Z,2))
RETURN(Z)
*END:DOLLARS
```

Comments:

This User-Defined Function uses the TRANSFORM function to display a number as a dollar amount, and the IIF command to place a minus sign in front of the dollar sign where necessary.

DAY-OF-THE-WEEK

The problem:

Throughout one application, I constantly had to display a date in the form Sunday December 7th, 1941.

The solution:

I created a User-Defined Function to perform this operation.

The calling code:

```
*    . . .
     SET COLOR TO &ColStand
     CLEAR
     X  =  {12/07/41}
     @ 11,20 SAY SPELLDAY(X)
     X  =  {06/30/80}
     @ 13,20 SAY SPELLDAY(X)
*    . . .
```

The User-Defined Function:

```
FUNCTION SPELLDAY
*
*|  Program...: SPELLDAY
*|  Author....: Phil Steele - President
*|             Phillipps Computer Systems Inc.
*|  Address...: 52 Hook Mountain Road,
*|             Montville NJ 07045
*|  Phone.....: (201) 575-8575
*|  Date......: 01/02/89
*|  Notice....: Copyright 1989  Philip Steele,
*|             All Rights Reserved.
*|  Notes.....: This procedure converts a date to
*|             words.
*|  Example...: 01/02/89 = Monday January 2nd 1989.
*|  Parameters: Express - The expression to convert.
*
PARAMETERS NDate
PRIVATE    NameDate,NameMon,SDay,SYear,NDay,NDay2,Suf
NameDay = CDOW(NDate)
NameMon = CMONTH(NDate)
SDay    = SUBSTR(DTOC(NDate),4,2)
SYear   = SUBSTR(DTOS(NDate),1,4)
NDay    = VAL(SDay)
NDay2   = VAL(SUBSTR(SDay,2,1))
SDay    = IIF(NDay<9, STR(NDay,1,0), SDay)
IF NDay > 3 .AND. NDay < 21
   Suf = "th"
ELSE
   Suf = SUBSTR("thstndrdthththththth", (NDay2*2)+1, 2)
ENDIF
RETURN(NameDay+" "+NameMon+" "+SDay+Suf+" "+SYear)
*END:SPELLDAY
```

Comments:

This User-Defined Function uses CDOW and CMONTH to produce the day of the week and month in alphabetic form. However, coming up with a successful method of getting the "st, nd, rd, and th" took some doing. Any day between 4 and 20 ends in **th**, as the 10th. The 1, 2, 21, 22 and 31 are the special cases and resolved with the statement:

"Suf = SUBSTR ("thstndrdthththththth",(NDAY2*2)+1,2)"

GRAPHING PROGRESS

The problem:

You are processing a large database (over 10,000 records). It takes three to five minutes to complete, and the user is upset because he only sees a blank screen, and he can't tell how far the processing has progressed.

The solution:

Use a general-purpose User-Defined Function to graphically reflect the progress of an operation.

The calling code:

```
*   . . .
SET COLOR TO W + /B,R + /B,B,B
CLEAR
A = Cent(12, 80, "P R O C E S S I N G")
@ 18,10 TO 23,69 DOUBLE
@ 21,11 TO 21,68 DOUBLE
@ 21,10 SAY "   "
@ 21,69 SAY "   "
@ 19,24 SAY "P E R C E N T    C O M P L E T E"
@ 20,14 SAY "0   10   20   30   40   50"
@ 20,44 SAY "60   70   80   90   100"
USE EMPLOYEE
TotalRec  =  RECCOUNT( )
SET COLOR TO R + /B,W + /B,B,B
GOTO TOP
DO WHILE .NOT. EOF( )
   A  =  BarGraph(TotalRec)
*   . . .
*   . . .
   Key  =   INKEY(1)
   SKIP
ENDDO
SET COLOR TO &ColStand
*   . . .
```

The User-Defined Function:

```
FUNCTION BARGRAPH
*┌──────────────────────────────────────────────────────────────┐
*│ Program...: BARGRAPH                                           │
*│ Author....: Phil Steele - President                           │
*│             Phillipps Computer Systems Inc.                   │
*│ Address...: 52 Hook Mountain Road,                            │
*│             Montville NJ 07045                                │
*│ Phone.....: (201) 575-8575                                    │
*│ Date......: 01/02/89                                          │
*│ Notice....: Copyright 1989  Philip Steele,                    │
*│             All Rights Reserved.                              │
*│ Notes.....: This function displays a bar graph                │
*│             depicting the progress of a DO WHILE              │
*│             or other sequential operation.                    │
*│ Parameters: Tot - Total number of records in the              │
*│                    database.                                  │
*└──────────────────────────────────────────────────────────────┘
PARAMETERS Tot
PRIVATE     Tot, Pct
IF RECNO() < Tot + 1
   Pct = RECNO() * 100 / Tot
   @ 22,14 SAY REPLICATE("█",(Pct/2)+1)    && CHR(219)
ENDIF
RETURN(.T.)
*END:BARGRAPH
```

Comments:

The calling sequence is as important as the UDF for the BARGRAPH. Because this function will be called many times, only the minimum amount of code should be placed in the UDF. The calling code sets the colors, draws the box in which the bar graph will appear, and places the headings in the box. The UDF computes the percentage based upon the current record number and the passed value in Tot. A line consisting of CHR(219) is placed in the pre-drawn box. One CHR(219) is drawn for each 2%—therefore, 100% consists of a line of fifty CHR(219)s.

HIDING THE CURSOR

The problem:

You are using a blinking arrow in place of the cursor. However, the cursor still appears on the screen, and confuses the user.

The solution:

Use a general-purpose User-Defined Function to hide the cursor.

The calling code:

```
*    . . .
     SET COLOR TO &ColStand
     CLEAR
     SET COLOR TO N/N
     @ 12,27 CLEAR TO 14,57
     SET COLOR TO &ColMenu
     @ 11,25 CLEAR TO 13,55
     @ 11,25    TO 13,55 DOUBLE
     @ 12,31 SAY "P R O C E S S I N G"
     Key   =   INKEY(0)
     A     =   HIDECUR(14,56)
     Key   =   INKEY(0)
     SET COLOR TO &ColStand
*    . . .
```

The User-Defined Function:

```
FUNCTION HIDECUR
*
* | Program...: HIDECUR
* | Author....: Phil Steele - President
* |             Phillipps Computer Systems Inc.
* | Address...: 52 Hook Mountain Road,
* |             Montville NJ 07045
* | Phone.....: (201) 575-8575
* | Date......: 01/02/89
* | Notice....: Copyright 1989  Philip Steele,
* |             All Rights Reserved.
* | Notes.....: This procedure hides the cursor by
* |             setting it to blank and placing it at
* |             a black area on the screen.
* | Parameters: X - Row of a black area on the screen.
* |             Y - Col of a black area on the screen.
*
PARAMETERS X, Y
SET COLOR TO X
@ X,Y SAY " "
RETURN(.T.)
*END:HIDECUR
```

Comments:

This UDF places a blank cursor in a black area on the screen (the location is passed by the calling program), and returns to the calling program.

SIMPLE MENUS

The problem:

> You are using many different menus in your system, and you are getting tired of using the new menu function of dBASE IV for creating simple menus. However, you want the ability to dress up your menus with borders and drop shadows, as necessary.

The solution:

> Use a Procedure to produce simple menus and return the user's selection.

The calling code:

```
*    . . .
     SET COLOR TO &ColStand
     CLEAR
     Ret     =   0
     SD      =   "D"
     Shadow  =   .T.
     BColor  =   "&ColMenu"
     Head    =   "MAIN MENU"
     NArray  =   7
     PUBLIC ARRAY MArray[7,2]
     MArray[1,1]   =   "A. This is an extra long prompt"
     MArray[2,1]   =   "B. Choice 2 "
     MArray[3,1]   =   "C. Choice 3 "
     MArray[4,1]   =   "D. Choice 4 "
     MArray[5,1]   =   "E. Choice 5 "
     MArray[6,1]   =   "F. Choice 6 "
     MArray[7,1]   =   "G. EXIT"
     MArray[1,2]   =   "Message for Choice 1"
     MArray[2,2]   =   "Message for Choice 2"
     MArray[3,2]   =   "Message for Choice 3"
     MArray[4,2]   =   "Message for Choice 4"
     MArray[5,2]   =   "Message for Choice 5"
     MArray[6,2]   =   "Message for Choice 6"
     MArray[7,2]   =   "Return to Main Menu"
     DO MEN WITH Head, NArray, Shadow, SD, BColor, Ret
     SET COLOR TO &ColStand
     @ 0,0 CLEAR TO 24,79
     @ 12,31 SAY "Your choice was: " + STR(Ret,1,0)
     @ 23,0 SAY " "
     WAIT
*    . . .
```

The Procedure:

```
PROCEDURE MEN
*
*   Program...: MEN
*   Author....: Phil Steele - President
*             Phillipps Computer Systems Inc.
*   Address...: 52 Hook Mountain Road,
*             Montville NJ 07045
*   Phone.....: (201) 575-8575
*   Date......: 01/02/89
*   Notice....: Copyright 1989  Philip Steele,
*             All Rights Reserved.
*   Notes.....: This function produces a centered
*             light bar menu with a surrounding
*             single or double box, a title and a
*             drop shadow if desired.
*   Parameters: Head   - The Heading for the menu.
*             MArray - A public array containing the
*                      prompts as the first element,
*                      [X,1] and the messages as the
*                      second element [X,2].
*                      DIMENSION [X,2]. (NOT PASSED)
*             NArray - The number of elements in the
*                      array.
*             Shadow - Should a shadow be drawn?
*             SD     - Draw a single "S", or double
*                      "D" box.
*             BC     - Color of the box.
*             Ret    - The menu selection to be
*                      returned.
*
PARAMETER Head, NArray, Shadow, SD, BC, Ret
PRIVATE T, L, B, R, N, Kind, LArr, NewLArr, SinDou,;
        EndBar1, EndBar2, EBS1, EBS2, EBD1, EBD2, Temp
EBS1 = CHR(198)       &&  ╞
EBS2 = CHR(181)       &&  ╡
EBD1 = CHR(199)       &&  ╟
EBD2 = CHR(182)       &&  ╢
IF SD ="S"
   EndBar1 = EBS1
   EndBar2 = EBS2
   SinDou  = "DOUBLE"
ELSE
   EndBar1 = EBD1
   EndBar2 = EBD2
   SinDou  = " "
ENDIF

*** Determine the maximum length of a Menu item ***
N    = 1
LArr = LEN(Head)
DO WHILE N <= NArray
   Temp    = MArray[N,1]
   NewLArr = LEN(Temp)
   LArr    = IIF(NewLArr>LArr, NewLArr, LArr)
```

```
   N          = N + 1
ENDDO

T = INT((20 - NArray) / 2) - 2
L = INT((80 - LArr)    / 2)
B = T + NArray + 3
R = L + LArr   + 3
*** Center the Header ***
Head = IIF(LArr>LEN(Head), SPACE((R-L-
LEN(Head))/2)+Head, Head)
SET COLOR TO &BC
DO NOWINBOX WITH T, L, B, R, SD, Shadow, "&BC"
@ T+2, L+1 TO T+2, R-1 &SinDou
@ T+2, L   SAY EndBar1
@ T+2, R   SAY EnDBar2
@ T+1, L+1 SAY Head
N = 1
DEFINE MENU Choose
N = 1
DO WHILE N <= NArray
   X = MArray[N,1]
   Y = "Y" + IIF(N<10, STR(N,1,0), STR(N,2,0))
   Z = MArray[N,2]
   DEFINE PAD &Y OF Choose PROMPT X AT T+N+2, L+1
MESSAGE "&Z"
   N = N + 1
   ON SELECTION PAD &Y OF Choose DO ChooseIt WITH Ret
ENDDO
ACTIVATE MENU Choose
RETURN
*END:MEN


PROCEDURE CHOOSEIT
PARAMETERS Choice
Choice = VAL(SUBSTR(PAD(),2,1))
DEACTIVATE MENU
RELEASE     MENU
RETURN
*END:CHOOSEIT
```

Comments:

This Procedure makes use of a PUBLIC double sub-
scripted array to contain the menu prompts and
messages. It creates a single or double box with room
for a heading (which is passed), and a drop shadow if
requested. The procedure determines the size of the box
based upon the larger of either the header or longest
prompt. The box looks like either:

```
+------------------+          +------------------+
|    HEAD AREA     |          |    HEAD AREA     |
+------------------+    or    +==================+
|                  |          |                  |
|                  |          |                  |
|                  |          |                  |
+------------------+          +------------------+
```

After the box is drawn, the menu is activated, and the
user makes a selection. Then the menu is deactivated
and released. The user's selection is returned to the
calling code. Note: This procedure uses NOWINBOX
which was defined previously, and ChooseIt, which is
included here. ChooseIt returns the number representing
the user's selection, and deactivates the menu. The
calling code must clear the screen and take action, depending upon the returned selection.

SELECT SCREEN COLORS

The problem:

You have just finished a large system and turned it over to the user—they love it! There is one problem, however. They do not like the colors you have chosen for most of the screens, and they would like you to change them all.

The solution:

If you defined all your colors up front and used the structure "SET COLOR TO & ColType" you can create a Procedure that will allow the user to change the colors of all the screens in the system—otherwise, you would have to change each "SET COLOR TO XX/XX" command in the system yourself.

The calling code:

```
*    . . .
     SET COLOR TO &ColStand
     CLEAR
     DO COLORS
     SET COLOR TO &ColStand
     CLEAR
*    . . .
```

The Procedure:

```
PROCEDURE COLORS
*
* | Program...: COLORS
* | Author....: Phil Steele - President
* |             Phillipps Computer Systems Inc.
* | Address...: 52 Hook Mountain Road,
* |             Montville NJ 07045
* | Phone.....: (201) 575-8575
* | Date......: 01/02/89
* | Notice....: Copyright 1989  Philip Steele,
* |             All Rights Reserved.
* | Notes.....: This procedure permits the user to
* |             change various screen colors at will.
* | Parameters: None.
* | Notes.....: You need a file called USER.MEM
* |             LISTING OF USER.MEM
* |   ColFunc    = "N/W"
* |   ColBlank   = "N/N,N/N,B,B"
* |   ColHelp    = "N/G,N/W,B,B"
* |   ColData    = "RG+/B,N/W,B,B"
* |   ColError   = "W+/R,W+/R,B,B"
* |   ColEntry   = "N/W,W+/N,B,B"
* |   ColStand   = "W+/B,N/W,B,B"
* |   ColMenu    = "RG+/R,N/W,B,B"
* |   ColWarning = "N/BG,W+/N,B,B"
*
* * * SECTION 1 * * *
SET COLOR TO &ColMenu
@ 14,6 CLEAR TO 23,22
@ 14,6        TO 23,22
@ 16,7        TO 16,22 DOUBLE
@ 16,6   SAY "╠"
@ 16,22  SAY "╣"
@ 15,12 SAY "MENU"
DEFINE MENU Colors
DEFINE PAD B OF Colors PROMPT "1. Background" AT 17,7
DEFINE PAD D OF Colors PROMPT "2. Data      " AT 18,7
DEFINE PAD H OF Colors PROMPT "3. Help      " AT 19,7
DEFINE PAD M OF Colors PROMPT "4. Menu      " AT 20,7
DEFINE PAD W OF Colors PROMPT "5. Warning   " AT 21,7
DEFINE PAD F OF Colors PROMPT "6. Return    " AT 22,7
ON SELECTION PAD B OF Colors DO CLRS WITH 1
ON SELECTION PAD D OF Colors DO CLRS WITH 2
ON SELECTION PAD H OF Colors DO CLRS WITH 3
ON SELECTION PAD M OF Colors DO CLRS WITH 4
ON SELECTION PAD W OF Colors DO CLRS WITH 5
ON SELECTION PAD F OF Colors DO Finished
ACTIVATE MENU Colors
RETURN
*END:COLORS
```

```
* * * SECTION 2 * * *
* ───────────────
PROCEDURE CLRS
* ───────────────
PARAMETERS BDHMW
Pass = 1
PUBLIC ARRAY mColArray[16]
RESTORE FROM USER ADDITIVE
mColArray [ 1] = "W+"
mColArray [ 2] = "W"
mColArray [ 3] = "RG+"
mColArray [ 4] = "RG"
mColArray [ 5] = "RB+"
mColArray [ 6] = "RB"
mColArray [ 7] = "R+"
mColArray [ 8] = "R"
mColArray [ 9] = "GB+"
mColArray [10] = "GB"
mColArray [11] = "G+"
mColArray [12] = "G"
mColArray [13] = "B+"
mColArray [14] = "B"
mColArray [15] = "N+"
mColArray [16] = "N"
STORE 6  TO X1,X2,HoldX,X
STORE 50 TO Y1,Y
STORE 65 TO Y2,HoldY
Forg  = "W+"
Bakg  = "W"
Active = "X"
DO ColDisp WITH Forg, Bakg, Active, X1, X2,;
               Y1, Y2, 9, Pass, BDHMW


* * * SECTION 3 * * *
DO WHILE .T.
   A   = HideCur(19,42)
   Key = INKEY(0)
   DO CASE
      CASE Key = CurDn .OR. Key = CurUp
         IF Active = "X"
            X = X1
            Y = Y1
         ELSE
            X = X2
            Y = Y2
         ENDIF
         X = IIF(Key = CurDn,X + 1,X - 1)
         X = IIF(Y = 65 .AND. X = 15,6,X)
         X = IIF(Y = 65 .AND. X = 5,14,X)
         X = IIF(Y = 50 .AND. X = 22,6,X)
         X = IIF(Y = 50 .AND. X = 5,21,X)
      CASE Key = CurRight
         SET COLOR TO W+/B
         @ X1,Y1 SAY "►"
         SET COLOR TO W+*/B
         @ HoldX,HoldY SAY "►"
```

```
                    X = HoldX
                    Y = HoldY
                    HoldX = X1
                    HoldY = 50
                    STORE 65 TO Y2,Y
                    Active = "Y"
                 CASE Key = CurLeft
                    SET COLOR TO W+/B
                    @ X2,Y2 SAY "►"
                    SET COLOR TO W+*/B
                    @ HoldX,HoldY SAY "►"
                    X = HoldX
                    Y = HoldY
                    HoldX = X2
                    HoldY = 65
                    STORE 50 TO Y1,Y
                    Active = "X"
                 CASE Key = Escape
                    EXIT
              ENDCASE

          * * * SECTION 4 * * *
             IF Active = "X"
                SET COLOR TO B/B
                @ X1,Y1 SAY " "
                X1 = X
                Y1 = Y
                SET COLOR TO W+*/B
                @ X1,Y1 SAY "►"
             ENDIF
             IF Active = "Y"
                SET COLOR TO B/B
                @ X2,Y2 SAY " "
                X2 = X
                Y2 = Y
                SET COLOR TO W+*/B
                @ X2,Y2 SAY "►"
             ENDIF
             DoIt = .T.
             IF Active = "Y" .AND. X2 = 14 .AND. Key = Enter
                DoIt       = .F.
                ColFunc    = "N/W"
                ColBlank   = "N/N,N/N,B,B"
                ColHelp    = "N/G,N/W,B,B"
                ColData    = "RG+/B,N/W,B,B"
                ColError   = "W+/R,W+/R,B,B"
                ColEntry   = "N/W,W+/N,B,B"
                ColStand   = "W+/B,N/W,B,B"
                ColMenu    = "RG+/R,N/W,B,B"
                ColWarning = "N/BG,W+/N,B,B"
                DO CASE
                   CASE BDHMW = 1
                       Forg = "W+/"
                       Bakg = "B"
                   CASE BDHMW = 2
                       Forg = "RG+/"
                       Bakg = "B"
```

```
            CASE BDHMW = 3
                Forg = "N/"
                Bakg = "G"
            CASE BDHMW = 4
                Forg = "RG+/"
                Bakg = "R"
            CASE BDHMW = 5
                Forg = "N/"
                Bakg = "BG"
         ENDCASE
         DO ColDisp WITH Forg, Bakg, Active, X1, X2,;
                         Y1, Y2, BDHMW, Pass, BDHMW
      ENDIF

 * * * SECTION 5 * * *
    IF Key = Enter
       SET COLOR TO W+*/R
       @ 17,66 SAY "    SAVING    "
       SAVE TO USER ALL LIKE Col*
       DoIt = .F.
       DO CASE
          CASE BDHMW = 1
             ColStand   = Forg + Bakg + ",N/W,B,B"
          CASE BDHMW = 2
             ColData    = Forg + Bakg + ",N/W,B,B"
          CASE BDHMW = 3
             ColHelp    = Forg + Bakg + ",N/W,B,B"
          CASE BDHMW = 4
             ColMenu    = Forg + Bakg + ",N/W,B,B"
          CASE BDHMW = 5
             ColWarning = Forg + Bakg + ",W+/N,B,B"
       ENDCASE
       Key = INKEY(1)
       SET COLOR TO W+/B
       @ 17,66 SAY "              "
       EXIT
    ENDIF

 * * * SECTION 6 * * *
    IF DoIt
       IF Key <> Enter
          Forg = mColArray[X1-5] + "/"
          IF X2 < 14
             Bakg = mColArray[(X2-5)*2]
          ENDIF
       ENDIF
       DO CASE
          CASE BDHMW = 1
             ColStand   = Forg + Bakg + ",N/W,B,B"
          CASE BDHMW = 2
             ColData    = Forg + Bakg + ",N/W,B,B"
          CASE BDHMW = 3
             ColHelp    = Forg + Bakg + ",N/W,B,B"
          CASE BDHMW = 4
             ColMenu    = Forg + Bakg + ",N/W,B,B"
          CASE BDHMW = 5
```

```
                        ColWarning = Forg + Bakg + ",W+/N,B,B"
              ENDCASE
              DO ColDisp WITH Forg, Bakg, Active, X1, X2,;
                           Y1, Y2, BDHMW, Pass, BDHMW
        ENDIF
ENDDO
SET COLOR TO &ColStand
DO NOARROW
RETURN
*END:CLRS.PRG

* * * SECTION 7 * * *
* ─────────────────
PROCEDURE COLDISP
* ─────────────────
PARAMETERS Forg, Bakg, Active, X1, X2,;
            Y1, Y2, Choice, Pass, BDHMW
NewCol = Forg + Bakg
IF Choice = 1                      && STANDARD COLOR
    SET COLOR TO &NewCol
ELSE
    SET COLOR TO &ColStand
ENDIF
@  3,0 CLEAR TO 23,47
@  3,18      TO  5,33
@  3,0 SAY "‖  ↑"
@  4,0 SAY "‖  "
@  5,0 SAY "‖  "
@  6,0 SAY "‖  Customer:"
@  7,0 SAY "‖  "
@  8,0 SAY "‖  Address :"
@  9,0 SAY "‖  "
@ 10,0 SAY "‖  City     :                        State:"
@ 11,0 SAY "‖  "
@ 12,0 SAY "‖  Phone   : (  )   -              Zi
@ 13,0 SAY "‖─│─↑──────────────────↑" +;
           "┘──────────────────"
@ 14,0 SAY "‖  │                      │"
@ 15,0 SAY "‖  │                      │"
@ 16,0 SAY "‖  │                      │"
@ 17,0 SAY "‖  └                      ┘"
@ 18,0 SAY "‖  │"
@ 19,0 SAY "‖  └                          ↑"
@ 20,0 SAY "‖                            │"
@ 21,0 SAY "‖                            └"
@ 22,0 SAY "‖ "
@ 23,0 SAY "└"
@ 23,1 TO 23,47 DOUBLE
@ 4,20 SAY "MAIN HEADING"


* * * SECTION 8 * * *
IF Choice = 2                      && DATA COLOR
    SET COLOR TO &NewCol
ELSE
    SET COLOR TO &ColData
ENDIF
```

```
@  6,13 SAY "Phillipps Computer Systems Inc."
@  8,13 SAY "52 Hook Mountain Road"
@ 10,13 SAY "Montville"
@ 10,41 SAY "NJ"
@ 12,14 SAY "201"
@ 12,18 SAY "575"
@ 12,22 SAY "8575"
@ 12,40 SAY " 07045"
SET COLOR TO N/N
@ 16,42 CLEAR TO 19,43
@ 19,30 CLEAR TO 19,43


* * * SECTION 9 * * *
IF Choice = 3                       && HELP COLOR
    SET COLOR TO &NewCol
ELSE
    SET COLOR TO &ColHelp
ENDIF
@ 0,0 SAY "╔══════════════════════╗" +;
          "══════════════════════"
@ 1,0 SAY "║    These are the help colors." +;
          "                  "
@ 2,0 SAY "╚══════════════════════╝" +;
          "══════════════════════"

* * * SECTION 10 * * *
IF Choice = 4                       && MENU COLOR
    SET COLOR TO &NewCol
ELSE
    SET COLOR TO &ColMenu
ENDIF
@ 14,6 SAY "┌─────────────┐      "
@ 15,6 SAY "│     MENU    │      "
@ 16,6 SAY "├─────────────┤      "
@ 17,6 SAY "├─1. Background │      "
@ 18,6 SAY "│  2. Data──────┤      "
@ 19,6 SAY "├─3. Help       │      "
@ 20,6 SAY "│  4. Menu      │      "
@ 21,6 SAY "│  5. Warning───┤      "
@ 22,6 SAY "│  6. Return    │      "
@ 23,6 SAY "└─────────────┘      "
SET COLOR TO &ColFunc
DO CASE
    CASE BDHMW = 1
       @ 17,7 SAY " 1. Background "
    CASE BDHMW = 2
       @ 18,7 SAY " 2. Data──────"
    CASE BDHMW = 3
       @ 19,7 SAY " 3. Help       "
    CASE BDHMW = 4
       @ 20,7 SAY " 4. Menu       "
    CASE BDHMW = 5
       @ 21,7 SAY " 5. Warning───"
ENDCASE
```

```
* * * SECTION 11 * * *
IF Choice = 5                        && WARNING COLOR
   SET COLOR TO &NewCol
ELSE
   SET COLOR TO &ColWarning
ENDIF
@ 15,28 TO 18,41
@ 16,29 SAY "  Warning    "
@ 17,29 SAY "   Colors    "

* * * SECTION 12 * * *
IF Pass = 1
   Pass = 2
   SET COLOR TO  &ColHelp
   @ 24,0 CLEAR TO 24,79
   @ 24,0 SAY "    Esc-return    ↑↓-up/down" +;
              "     -background    -foreground" +;
              "     -reset/save"
   SET COLOR TO  &ColFunc
   @ 24,4 SAY "ESC"
   @ 24,17 SAY "↑↓"
   @ 24,32 SAY CHR(26)              && -▸
   @ 24,47 SAY CHR(27)              && ◂-
   @ 24,61 SAY "◂—⌐ "
   SET COLOR TO W+/B,W+/B,B,B  && CHOICES
   @ 0,48 CLEAR TO 23,79
   @ 0,48         TO 23,79
   @ 0,48 SAY " ═════ SCREEN COLOR ═════⌐ "
   @ 2,52 SAY "SELECT COLORS COMBINATIONS"
   @ 4,52 SAY "Foreground    Background"
   @ 5,52 SAY "───────    ───────"
   SET COLOR TO W+/B
   @  6,52 SAY "HI WHITE     "
   Forg = "W+"
   SET COLOR TO W/B
   @  7,52 SAY "WHITE        "
   Forg = "W"
   SET COLOR TO RG+/B
   @  8,52 SAY "HI YELLOW    "
   Forg = "RG+"
   SET COLOR TO RG/B
   @  9,52 SAY "BROWN        "
   Forg = "RG"
   SET COLOR TO RB+/B
   @ 10,52 SAY "HI MAGENTA   "
   Forg = "RB+"
   SET COLOR TO RB/B
   @ 11,52 SAY "MAGENTA      "
   Forg = "RB"
   SET COLOR TO R+/B
   @ 12,52 SAY "HI RED       "
   Forg = "R+"
   SET COLOR TO R/B
   @ 13,52 SAY "RED          "
   Forg = "R"
   SET COLOR TO GB+/B
```

```
@ 14,52 SAY "HI CYAN         "
Forg = "GB+"
SET COLOR TO GB/B
@ 15,52 SAY "CYAN            "
Forg = "GB"
SET COLOR TO G+/B
@ 16,52 SAY "HI GREEN        "
Forg = "G+"
SET COLOR TO G/B
@ 17,52 SAY "GREEN           "
Forg = "G"
SET COLOR TO B+/B
@ 18,52 SAY "HI BLUE         "
Forg = "B+"
    SET COLOR TO B/B
    @ 19,52 SAY "BLUE            "
    Forg = "B"
    SET COLOR TO N+/B
    @ 20,52 SAY "HI BLACK        "
    Forg = "N+"
    SET COLOR TO N/B
    @ 21,52 SAY "BLACK           "
    Forg = "N"
    SET COLOR TO  /W
    Bakg = "W"
    @  6,66 SAY "WHITE           "
    SET COLOR TO  /RG
    Bakg = "RG"
    @  7,66 SAY "BROWN           "
    SET COLOR TO  /RB
    Bakg = "RB"
    @  8,66 SAY "MAGENTA         "
    SET COLOR TO  /R
    Bakg = "R"
    @  9,66 SAY "RED             "
    SET COLOR TO  /GB
    Bakg = "GB"
    @ 10,66 SAY "CYAN            "
    SET COLOR TO  /G
    Bakg = "G"
    @ 11,66 SAY "GREEN           "
    SET COLOR TO  /B
    Bakg = "B"
    @ 12,66 SAY "BLUE            "
    SET COLOR TO  /N
    Bakg = "N"
    @ 13,66 SAY "BLACK           "
    SET COLOR TO N/W
    @ 14,66 SAY "RESET ORIG."
ENDIF
IF Active = "X"
    SET COLOR TO W+*/B
    @ X1,Y1 SAY "►"
    SET COLOR TO W+/B
    @ X2,Y2 SAY "►"
ELSE
```

```
          SET COLOR TO W+*/B
          @ X2,Y2 SAY "►"
          SET COLOR TO W+/B
          @ X1,Y1 SAY "►"
ENDIF
A = HideCur(19,42)
RETURN
*EOF:COLDISP

* * * SECTION 13 * * *
* ─────────────────
PROCEDURE NOARROW
* ─────────────────
SET COLOR TO W+/B
X = 5
DO WHILE X < 22
    X = X + 1
    @ X,50 SAY " "
    IF X < 15
       @ X,65 SAY " "
    ENDIF
ENDDO
RETURN
*END:NOARROW

* * * SECTION 14 * * *
* ─────────────────
PROCEDURE FINISHED
* ─────────────────
DEACTIVATE MENU
RELEASE    MENU
SET COLOR TO &ColStand
RETURN TO MASTER
*END:FINISHED
```

Comments:

Now look at this code to see how it works. Because it is fairly long, look at the code a section at a time. Each section is delimited with the comment line:
"* * * SECTION 1 * * *" etc., etc.

Section 1 & 14—This Procedure places a menu enclosed in a box at the bottom left of the screen. This menu permits the user to change the colors of the following screen areas or types:

Background
Data
Help
Menu
Warning

The menu calls the procedure CLRS with a number indicating one of the five screen areas or types. The deactivating and closing of the menu (choice = 5) is done in section 14. The return to master command is included so that normal processing can resume after the new colors are selected.

Note 1—The positioning of each menu choice on the initial screen is the same as on the color screen. If either screen or position is changed, then the other must be changed. This Procedure is designed to be selected from a higher level menu that performs other "utility" type functions, such as accessing DOS or changing other parameters such as the date or time.

Note 2—This User-Defined Function updates a memory file called USER.MEM which must be manually set the first time. (Copy the comments starting after USER.MEM, make them dBASE IV statements, add the line "SAVE TO USER" and run this mini program).

Section 2—The procedure CLRS restores User.MEM—just in case it was not done from the calling procedure. (Remember, you may implement this differently than shown here). Next, the procedure CLRS sets the variable "Pass" to 1 and declares the array mColArray public. It fills the array with the 16 possible colors available for a CGA display. Local variables are initialized, as well as colors for the initial menu choices. The procedure ColDisp is called which displays the initial screen permitting the user to select the color combinations wanted. Note: If you will always be using an EGA or VGA display, and wish to use more lines per screen or more colors, you will have to change this function and this array.

Section 7—Because ColDisp is called next, look at Section 7. The passed parameters include: the desired foreground and background colors (Forg, Bakg); the active area (X = foreground, Y = background); the cursor positions for the foreground and background arrows (X1, X2, Y1, Y2); the current color choice for the area of the screen to change (Choice 1-5); the pass number (Pass); and the current menu selection indicating the area of the screen to change (BDHMW). NewCol (the active color) is set equal to the passed foreground and background colors. If the selected area is the background area (choice = 1), the background color is set to NewCol—otherwise, the background area is set to ColStand. The background portion of the screen is then redrawn.

Section 8—If the selected area is the data area (choice = 2), the data color is set to NewCol—otherwise, the data area is set to ColData. The data portion of the screen is then redrawn.

Section 9—If the selected area is the help area (choice = 3), the help color is set to NewCol—otherwise, the help area is set to ColHelp. The help portion of the screen is then redrawn.

Section 10—If the selected area is the menu area (choice = 4), the menu color is set to NewCol—otherwise, the menu area is set to ColMenu. The menu portion of the screen is then redrawn.

Section 11—If the selected area is the warning area (choice = 5), the warning color is set to NewCol—otherwise the warning area is set to ColWarning. The warning portion of the screen is then redrawn.

Section 12—If this is the first time the selection screen is drawn (Pass = 1), the color bar section of the screen is drawn. The proper arrow is made to blink and the cursor is hidden. Now let's return to the calling code.

Section 3—This is the main control sequence. Note that this is implemented as a DO WHILE .T. loop, which may seem confusing if you have never used this construct before. You may ask how to get out of this loop without using the Escape key? The answer is really quite simple: use the EXIT command when you wish to leave the loop. This is advantageous because you can exit at any point without having to resort to awkward programming techniques. Because dBASE IV doesn't contain a SET CURSOR OFF statement like Clipper Summer '87, we have to hide the cursor to simulate turning it off (see the User-Defined Function HIDECUR). This UDF is used to simulate turning the cursor off. The colors are set to blank-on-blank, and the cursor is placed over a blank area on the screen—this effectively turns the cursor off. Beware! If an error should occur after this function is performed, you will be unable to read the error message because it will be displayed as blank on a blank background. The code now waits to process a keystroke that will be sitting in the variable "Key". The possible choices and actions occur in the DO CASE statement. First, I check to see if the up-arrow or down-arrow key has been pressed. The active area X (foreground) or Y (background) is determined, and the value of X and Y is set. This permits us to "move" the arrow by writing a blank at the current location, changing the value of the row and column, and rewriting the arrow at the new location. The CASE where Key = CurRight selects the background color, and is indicated by turning the blinking bit off for the foreground arrow, and on for the background arrow. The current location of the inactive arrow is saved in HoldX and HoldY, and X and Y are set to the location of the active arrow. Active is set to "Y" to indicate that the background color is selected. The CASE where Key = CurLeft selects the foreground color, and is indicated by turning the blinking bit off for the background arrow and on for the foreground arrow. The current location of the inactive arrow is saved in HoldX and HoldY, and X and Y are set to the location of the active arrow. Active is set to "X" to indicate that the foreground color is selected. If the escape key is pressed (CASE Key = Escape), then processing is ended and control returned to the calling procedure. These are the only keys processed in the CASE construct which ends here.

Section 4—If "Active" equals "X" then the cursor is moved (as previously described) if the foreground selection is active. If "Active" equals "Y" then the cursor is moved (as previously described) if the background selection is active. If the Enter key is pressed with the background active, the cursor on line 14 (restore original), and DoIt TRUE, then we reset the original colors and set DoIt to FALSE. Note: If you wish to establish a different set of "original" colors than I established, change the code here. Next, change the active area on the screen to the default (original) colors, and redisplay the screen with the original colors for the chosen section.

Section 5—If the Enter key has been pressed, the colors are set to those chosen, and tell the user that the current selections are being saved. The chosen colors are "SAVED" in the memory file USER.MEM, and the flag DoIT is set to FALSE to indicate that they have been saved. The selected area of the screen is set to the colors chosen, and three seconds are allowed to elapse before turning off the blinking message "SAVING". Control is returned to the calling procedure.

Section 6—If the current selection is not saved, then I set the colors to those indicated by the position of the arrows and display the screen with the current colors. The colors are set to the "standard color," the arrows are turned off by writing a blank to each position that can possibly contain an arrow—which indicates that additional color selections cannot be made—and control is returned to the calling procedure.

TURNING OFF THE CURSOR

The problem:

In the previous User-Defined Function "COLORS" we have set the cursor color to blank and put it on a black part of the display to "turn is off". There has to be a better way!

The solution:

Write a User-Defined Function to turn the cursor off. Most copies of PC-DOS come with a program called DEBUG which permits you to assemble assembly language code. You can use DEBUG to implement this User-Defined Function in assembly language.

The calling code:

```
*    . . .
     SET COLOR TO &ColStand
     CLEAR
     LOAD CURSOROF
     CALL CURSOROF
     @ 20,35 SAY " "
     WAIT
*    . . .
```

The User-Defined Function:

```
FUNCTION CURSOROF.BIN
*
*    Program...: CURSOROF.BIN
*    Author....: Phil Steele - President
*               Phillipps Computer Systems Inc.
*    Address...: 52 Hook Mountain Road,
*               Montville NJ 07045
*    Phone.....: (201) 575-8575
*    Date......: 01/02/89
*    Notice....: Copyright 1989  Philip Steele,
*               All Rights Reserved.
*    Notes.....: This function is written in assembler
*               and entered with DEBUG.
*               It turns the cursor off.
*    Parameters: NONE
*    Usage....:  LOAD CURSOROF - done once.
*               CALL CURSOROF
*
DEBUG                 ; AT DOS prompt enter the command DEBUG
N CURSOROF.BIN        ; tell debug the name of the program
A 100                 ; start assembly at Hex 100
PUSH AX               ; save AX - start of code
PUSH CX               ; save CX
MOV   AH,01           ; set BIOS service 01 - cursor
MOV   CH,20           ; Set bit 5 on - turn off cursor
INT   10              ; call ROM-BIOS video services
POP   CX              ; restore CX
POP   AX              ; restore AX
RETF                  ; return to dBASE IV - end of code
                      ; blank line to debug to stop assembly
R CX                  ; get register CX
0B                    ; tell it the code is 11 bytes (hex 0B)
W                     ; write the code
Q                     ; quit debug
```

Comments:

You can turn the cursor off and on using assembly language programs. I do not like to include assembly language programs in a book devoted to programming in dBASE IV, but controlling the cursor is extremely important. In most professional systems, you never see the cursor on the screen except when data entry is in progress. Take a tip from the pros and write your systems using the same approach. Because of the importance of cursor control, I am including two extra User-Defined Functions written in assembler language to control the cursor (CursorOf and CursorOn).

To use this User-Defined Function, you must create it using the DEBUG program supplied with most versions of PC-DOS. Enter all the commands as shown without the comments. The comments are from the semicolon to the end of the line, including the semicolon. Make sure to enter the blank line after RETF because this tells the debugger to stop assembling code.

After the file CURSOROF.BIN has been created, you must load it into dBASE IV. I usually put it at the beginning of the system—right after the SET commands in the preamble.

Whenever you wish to turn the cursor off, issue the dBASE IV command:

CALL CURSOROF

The cursor will vanish. Now you need a way to turn it back on which leads to our next User-Defined Function.

TURNING ON THE CURSOR

The problem:

In the previous User-Defined Function CURSOROF we turned off the cursor—now we need a method to turn the cursor back on.

The solution:

Write a User-Defined Function to turn the cursor on.

The calling code:

```
*    . . .
     SET COLOR TO &ColStand
     CLEAR
     LOAD CURSORON
     CALL CURSORON
     @ 20,35 SAY " "
      WAIT
*    . . .
```

The User-Defined Function:

```
FUNCTION CURSORON.BIN
*
* | Program...: CURSORON.BIN
* | Author....: Phil Steele - President
* |            Phillipps Computer Systems Inc.
* | Address...: 52 Hook Mountain Road,
* |            Montville NJ 07045
* | Phone.....: (201) 575-8575
* | Date......: 01/02/89
* | Notice....: Copyright 1989  Philip Steele,
* |            All Rights Reserved.
* | Notes.....: This function is written in assembler
* |            and entered with DEBUG.
* |            It turns the cursor on.
* | Parameters: NONE
* | Usage.....: LOAD CURSORON - done once.
* |            CALL CURSORON
*
DEBUG                 ; AT DOS prompt enter the command DEBUG
N CURSORON.BIN        ; tell debug the name of the program
A 100                 ; start assembly at Hex 100
PUSH AX               ; save AX - start of code
PUSH CX               ; save CX
INT  11               ; call ROM-BIOS service 11-get equipment
AND  AL,10            ; check to see if monochrome - bit 4 on
MOV  CX,0607          ; set cursor on in color mode
JZ   010E             ; if color (bit 4 off) skip next instr.
MOV  CX,0C0D          ; set cursor on in monochrome mode
MOV  AH,01            ; set BIOS service 01 - cursor
INT  10               ; call ROM-BIOS video services
POP  CX               ; restore CX
POP  AX               ; restore AX
RETF                  ; return to dBASE IV - end of code
                      ; blank line to debug to stop assembly
R CX                  ; get register CX
15                    ; tell it the code is 21 bytes (hex 15)
W                     ; write the code
Q                     ; quit debug
```

Comments:

To use this User-Defined Function, you must create it using the DEBUG program supplied with most versions of PC-DOS. Enter all the commands as shown without the comments. The comments are from the semicolon to the end of the line, including the semicolon.

Make sure to enter the blank line after RETF: this tells the debugger to stop assembling code.

After the file CURSORON.BIN has been created you must load it into dBASE IV. I usually put it at the beginning of the system—right after the SET commands in the preamble.

Whenever you wish to turn the cursor on, issue the dBASE IV command:

CALL CURSORON

The cursor will reappear if it was previously turned off.

3

Computation

Webster's Ninth New Collegiate Dictionary defines "computation" as: "the use or operation of a computer." Indeed, computation is the original use of electronic computers (to create trajectory tables for the navy). In this chapter, I describe functions that are central to computer computations. Though binary arithmetic is used internally in all modern computers, the binary digits (Bytes) are usually represented as hexadecimal numbers. Conversions between decimal and hexadecimal, and division by zero, are classic problems programmers deal with constantly.

This chapter presents unique algorithms to solve these classic problems.

DEC TO HEX

The problem:

You need to convert decimal numbers to hexadecimal numbers for a system you are developing.

The solution:

Use a general-purpose User-Defined Function to perform the conversion.

The calling code:

```
*   . . .
    SET COLOR TO &ColStand
    CLEAR
    DecNum  = 43690
    Hex     = HexEquiv(DecNum)
    ? Hex
*   The Hexadecimal equivalent is AAAA
*   . . .
```

The User-Defined Function:

```
FUNCTION HEXEQUIV
*
*   Program...: HEXEQUIV
*   Author....: Phil Steele - President
*              Phillipps Computer Systems Inc.
*   Address...: 52 Hook Mountain Road,
*              Montville NJ 07045
*   Phone.....: (201) 575-8575
*   Date......: 01/02/89
*   Notice....: Copyright 1989  Philip Steele,
*              All Rights Reserved.
*   Notes.....: This function converts a decimal
*              number (0-65535) to a hexadecimal
*              number.
*   Parameters: DecNum - The decimal number to be
*                        converted into a hexadecimal
*                        number.
*
PARAMETERS DecN
PRIVATE Ans, N1, N2, N3, N4, M1, M2, M3
N1 = INT(DecN / 4096)
M1 = N1 * 4096
N2 = INT((DecN - M1) / 256)
M2 = N2 * 256
N3 = INT((DecN - M1 - M2) / 16)
M3 = N3 * 16
N4 = INT(DecN - M1 - M2 - M3)
Ans = Let(N1) + Let(N2) + Let(N3) + Let(N4)
RETURN(Ans)
*END:HEXEQUIV
```

```
FUNCTION LET
*┌─────────────────────────────────────────────────────┐
*│ Program...: LET                                       │
*│ Author....: Phil Steele - President                   │
*│             Phillipps Computer Systems Inc.           │
*│ Address...: 52 Hook Mountain Road,                    │
*│             Montville NJ 07045                        │
*│ Phone.....: (201) 575-8575                            │
*│ Date......: 01/02/89                                  │
*│ Notice....: Copyright 1989  Philip Steele,            │
*│             All Rights Reserved.                      │
*│ Notes.....: This function converts the numbers        │
*│             0-15 to the string "0-9" / "A-F".         │
*│ Parameters: Num - The number to be converted to a     │
*│                   string.                             │
*│                                                       │
*└─────────────────────────────────────────────────────┘
PARAMETER Num
IF Num < 10 .AND. Num > 0
   RETURN(STR(Num,1,0))
ENDIF
DO CASE
   CASE Num = 0
      RETURN("0")
   CASE Num = 10
      RETURN("A")
   CASE Num = 11
      RETURN("B")
   CASE Num = 12
      RETURN("C")
   CASE Num = 13
      RETURN("D")
   CASE Num = 14
      RETURN("E")
   CASE Num = 15
      RETURN("F")
ENDCASE
*END:LET
```

Comments:

> HEXEQUIV parses the decimal number into its hexadecimal parts, and then calls a second UDF (LET) to convert the numbers 0 through 15 to "0" through "F" characters. These characters are concatenated into a hexadecimal number and returned to the calling procedure.

HEX TO DEC

The problem:

You need to convert hexadecimal numbers to decimal numbers for a system you are developing.

The solution:

Use a general-purpose User-Defined Function to perform the conversion.

The calling code:

```
*   . . .
    SET COLOR TO &ColStand
    CLEAR
    HexNum  =  "AAAA"
    Dec     =  DecEquiv(HexNum)
    ? Dec
*   The Decimal equivalent is 43690
*   . . .
```

The User-Defined Function:

```
FUNCTION DECEQUIV
*
*   Program...: DECEQUIV
*   Author....: Phil Steele - President
*               Phillipps Computer Systems Inc.
*   Address...: 52 Hook Mountain Road,
*               Montville NJ 07045
*   Phone.....: (201) 575-8575
*   Date......: 01/02/89
*   Notice....: Copyright 1989  Philip Steele,
*               All Rights Reserved.
*   Notes.....: This function converts a hexadecimal
*               number (0-FFFF) to a decimal number.
*   Parameters: HexNum - The hexadecimal number to be
*                        converted into a decimal
*                        number.
*
PARAMETERS HexN
PRIVATE Ans, AllHex, N1, N2, N3, N4
AllHex = "123456789ABCDEF"
N1 = AT(SUBSTR(HexN,1,1), AllHex)
N2 = AT(SUBSTR(HexN,2,1), AllHex)
N3 = AT(SUBSTR(HexN,3,1), AllHex)
N4 = AT(SUBSTR(HexN,4,1), AllHex)
Ans = (N1 * 4096) + (N2 * 256) + (N3 * 16) + N4
RETURN(Ans)
*END:DECEQUIV
```

Comments:

This UDF uses the SUBSTR function to extract a hexadecimal element and multiply it by the appropriate factor. These converted elements are combined into a decimal number and returned to the calling procedure.

DIVISION BY ZERO

The problem:

> While dividing various input quantities by other input quantities, you have forgotten to provide a check for division by zero, thus crashing the system.

The solution:

> Create a User-Defined Function to avoid division-by-zero problems.

The calling code:

```
*   . . .
    SET COLOR TO &ColStand
    CLEAR
    X  =  3
    Y  =  6
    Z  =  DIV(Y,X)
    ?Z              && 2
    X  =  0
    Z  =  DIV(Y,X)
    ?Z              && 0
    X  =  3
    Y  =  0
    Z  =  DIV(Y,X)
    ?Z              && 0
    X  =  0
    Y  =  0
    Z  =  DIV(Y,X)
    ?Z              && 0
*   . . .
```

The User-Defined Function:

```
FUNCTION DIV
*
*┌─────────────────────────────────────────────────────────┐
*│ Program...: DIV                                           │
*│ Author....: Phil Steele - President                       │
*│             Phillipps Computer Systems Inc.               │
*│ Address...: 52 Hook Mountain Road,                        │
*│             Montville NJ 07045                            │
*│ Phone.....: (201) 575-8575                                │
*│ Date......: 01/02/89                                      │
*│ Notice....: Copyright 1989  Philip Steele,                │
*│             All Rights Reserved.                          │
*│ Notes.....: This checks to see if a number is             │
*│             divided by zero and if so returns zero.       │
*│ Parameters: X - The numerator.                            │
*│             Y - The denominator.                          │
*└─────────────────────────────────────────────────────────┘
PARAMETERS X, Y
PRIVATE    X, Y
RETURN IIF(X=0 .OR. Y=0, 0, X/Y)
*END:DIV
```

Comments:

This UDF checks for a zero numerator or denominator and returns a zero if either is zero—otherwise, it performs the division.

ELAPSED TIME

The problem:

You are testing two algorithms that perform the same function, and you need to know which is faster. You try to time them with a stop watch, but the error introduced by starting and stopping the watch is too great.

The solution:

Develop a User-Defined Function that computes elapsed time.

The calling code:

```
*    . . .
  SET COLOR TO &ColStand
  CLEAR
  X  =  "14:32:21"       && Time1
  Y  =  "17:18:06"       && Time2
  Z  =  ElapTime(X,Y)
  ? Z
*   Elap Time  =  2:45:45
*   . . .
```

The User-Defined Function:

```
FUNCTION ELAPTIME
*┌──────────────────────────────────────────────────────┐
*│ Program...: ELAPTIME                                  │
*│ Author....: Phil Steele - President                  │
*│             Phillipps Computer Systems Inc.          │
*│ Address...: 52 Hook Mountain Road,                   │
*│             Montville NJ 07045                        │
*│ Phone.....: (201) 575-8575                            │
*│ Date......: 01/02/89                                  │
*│ Notice....: Copyright 1989  Philip Steele,           │
*│             All Rights Reserved.                     │
*│ Notes.....: This function computes the difference    │
*│             between time one and time two.           │
*│ Parameters: X  - String containing time one.         │
*│             Y  - String containing time two.         │
*└──────────────────────────────────────────────────────┘
PARAMETERS X, Y
PRIVATE  Time1, Time2, Z, Hrs, Min, Sec
Time1 = (VAL(SUBSTR(X,1,2)) * 3600) +;
        (VAL(SUBSTR(X,4,2)) * 60) + (VAL(SUBSTR(X,7)))
Time2 = (VAL(SUBSTR(Y,1,2)) * 3600) +;
        (VAL(SUBSTR(Y,4,2)) * 60) + (VAL(SUBSTR(Y,7)))
Z     = ABS(Time1 - Time2)
Hrs   = INT(Z / 3600)
Min   = INT((Z - Hrs * 3600) / 60)
Sec   = Z - (Hrs * 3600) - (Min * 60)
RETURN (LTRIM(STR(Hrs,4,0) + ":" + STR(Min,2,0) +;
        ":" + Str(Sec,2,0)))
*END:ELAPTIME
```

Comments:

This User-Defined Function converts Time1 and Time2 into seconds, subtracts one from the other, converts a negative result to positive, and reconverts the elapsed seconds back to hours, minutes and seconds.

ODDNESS

The problem:

You are creating an algorithms that depends upon the result of various calculations being odd. You need to test this condition many times in the algorithm.

The solution:

Develop a User-Defined Function that determines if a number is odd.

The calling code:

```
*  . . .
   SET COLOR TO &ColStand
   CLEAR
   X  =  - 23
   Y  =  ODD(X)
   ? Y              && .T.
   X  =  - 222
   Y  =  ODD(X)
   ? Y && .F.
*  . . .
```

The User-Defined Function:

```
FUNCTION ODD
*
*   Program...: ODD
*   Author....: Phil Steele - President
*             Phillipps Computer Systems Inc.
*   Address...: 52 Hook Mountain Road,
*             Montville NJ 07045
*   Phone.....: (201) 575-8575
*   Date......: 01/02/89
*   Notice....: Copyright 1989  Philip Steele,
*             All Rights Reserved.
*   Notes.....: This function returns .T. if it is
*             passed an odd number and .F. if it is
*             passed an even number.
*   Parameters: Num - The passed number to check to
*                     see if it is odd.
*
PARAMETERS Num
PRIVATE Ret
Ret = IIF(MOD(Num,2)=0, .F., .T.)
RETURN(Ret)
*END:ODD
```

Comments:

This User-Defined Function uses the MOD function
to determine if a number is odd, and returns TRUE
if it is.

EVENNESS

The problem:

You are creating an algorithm that depends upon the results of various calculations being even. You need to test this condition many times in the algorithm.

The solution:

Develop a User-Defined Function that determines if a number is even.

The calling code:

```
*  . . .
   SET COLOR TO &ColStand
   CLEAR
   X  =  - 23
   Y  =  ODD(X)
   ? Y            && .T.
   X  =  - 222
   Y  =  ODD(X)
   ? Y            && .T.
*  . . .
```

The User-Defined Function:

```
FUNCTION EVEN
*
* Program...: EVEN
* Author....: Phil Steele - President
*             Phillipps Computer Systems Inc.
* Address...: 52 Hook Mountain Road,
*             Montville NJ 07045
* Phone.....: (201) 575-8575
* Date......: 01/02/89
* Notice....: Copyright 1989  Philip Steele,
*             All Rights Reserved.
* Notes.....: This function returns .T. if it is
*             passed an even number and .T. if it is
*             passed an odd number.
* Parameters: Num - The passed number to check to
*                 see if it is even.
*
PARAMETERS Num
PRIVATE Ret
Ret = IIF(MOD(Num,2)=0, .T., .F.)
RETURN(Ret)
*END:EVEN
```

Comments:

This User-Defined Function uses the MOD function to determine if a number is even, and returns TRUE if it is.

4

Mathematical and Array Functions

Most of the time you only place needed calculations in the body of your code. If you need these calculations in more than one place, then put them in a User-Defined Function or Procedure. You then have the ability to use the calculations from various places in your code.

With the advent of dBASE IV, Ashton-Tate has finally given us "arrays." However, they provided very few functions that use these arrays. This chapter rectifies this condition. You cannot, however, use arrays in functions—therefore, all User-Defined Functions must be written as procedures.

FACTORIAL

The problem:

You have a user who needs to perform complex calculations in his application. One of these calculations requires the factorial function.

The solution:

The following User-Defined Function performs the factorial operation.

The calling code:

```
*  . . .
   SET COLOR TO &ColStand
   CLEAR
   N = 5
   Z = FACT(N)
   ? Z
*  . . .
```

The User-Defined Function:

```
FUNCTION FACT
*
*   Program...: FACT
*   Author....: Phil Steele - President
*             Phillipps Computer Systems Inc.
*   Address...: 52 Hook Mountain Road,
*             Montville NJ 07045
*   Phone.....: (201) 575-8575
*   Date......: 01/02/89
*   Notice....: Copyright 1989  Philip Steele,
*             All Rights Reserved.
*   Notes.....: This function computes the factorial
*             of a number.
*   Parameters: N - The number you need the factorial
*             of.
*
PARAMETERS N
PRIVATE    N, J, K
K = 1
J = 2
DO WHILE J <= N
   K = K * J
   J = J + 1
ENDDO
RETURN(K)
*END:FACT
```

Comments:

This UDF is straightforward and uses a DO WHILE loop to compute the factorial.

SUMMING ARRAYS

The problem:

You have a client who is working with arrays and statistics all the time, and who needs a series of functions to operate on these arrays. First you have to sum all the elements in the array.

The solution:

Use a Procedure to sum the elements of an array.

The calling code:

```
*  . . .
   SET COLOR TO &ColStand
   CLEAR
   PUBLIC ARRAY ArrayN[10]
   ArrayN[1]  =  87
   ArrayN[2]  =  79
   ArrayN[3]  =  97
   ArrayN[4]  =  83
   ArrayN[5]  =  90
   ArrayN[6]  =  85
   ArrayN[7]  =  51
   ArrayN[8]  =  98
   ArrayN[9]  =  99
   ArrayN[10] =  88
   TheSum     =  0
   DO ASum WITH "ArrayN", 10, TheSum
   ? TheSum PICTURE "999.99"
*  The Sum of the array  =  857.0
*   . . .
```

The Procedure:

```
PROCEDURE ASUM
*
*   Program...: ASUM
*   Author....: Phil Steele - President
*             Phillipps Computer Systems Inc.
*   Address...: 52 Hook Mountain Road,
*             Montville NJ 07045
*   Phone.....: (201) 575-8575
*   Date......: 01/02/89
*   Notice....: Copyright 1989  Philip Steele,
*             All Rights Reserved.
*   Notes.....: This function sums the elements of an
*             array.
*   Parameters: AName - The name of an array
*                     containing numeric elements to
*                     sum, the array must be
*                     declared public.
*           J   - The number of elements to sum.
*           Tot - The sum of the elements.
*
PARAMETERS AName, J, Tot
PRIVATE N, Tot, AName
Tot = 0
N   = 1
DO WHILE N <= J
   Tot = Tot + &AName[N]
   N   = N   + 1
ENDDO
RETURN
*END:ASUM
```

Comments:

This UDF uses a DO WHILE loop to sum the elements of the passed array, and returns the sum.

AVERAGING ARRAYS

The problem:

>You have a client who is working with arrays and statistics all the time, and who needs a series of functions to operate on these arrays. First, you have to sum all the elements in the array. After you have completed the function to sum the elements in the array, you need another function to compute the average (mean) of the elements in an array.

The solution:

>Use a Procedure to sum the elements of an array.

The calling code:

```
*  . . .
   SET COLOR TO &ColStand
   CLEAR
   PUBLIC ARRAY ArrayN[10]
   ArrayN[1]   = 87
   ArrayN[2]   = 79
   ArrayN[3]   = 97
   ArrayN[4]   = 83
   ArrayN[5]   = 90
   ArrayN[6]   = 85
   ArrayN[7]   = 51
 ⸱ ArrayN[8]   = 98
   ArrayN[9]   = 99
   ArrayN[10] = 88
   Mean        = 0
   DO AAvg WITH "ArrayN",10,Mean
   ? Mean PICTURE "999.99"
*  The Avg of the array  = 85.70
*  . . .
```

The Procedure:

```
PROCEDURE AAVG
*
*   Program...: AAVG
*   Author....: Phil Steele - President
*             Phillipps Computer Systems Inc.
*   Address...: 52 Hook Mountain Road,
*             Montville NJ 07045
*   Phone.....: (201) 575-8575
*   Date......: 01/02/89
*   Notice....: Copyright 1989  Philip Steele,
*             All Rights Reserved.
*   Notes.....: This function computes the average of
*             the elements in the array.
*   Parameters: AName - The name of an array
*                     containing numeric elements to
*                     average, the array must be
*                     declared public.
*             J     - The number of elements to
*                     average.
*             Avg   - The average.
*
PARAMETERS AName, J, Avg
PRIVATE N, Tot, Avg, AName
STORE 0 TO Tot, Avg
N = 1
DO WHILE N <= J
   Tot = Tot + &AName[N]
   N   = N   + 1
ENDDO
Avg = DIV(Tot, J)
RETURN
*END:AAVG
```

Comments:

This UDF uses a DO WHILE loop to sum the elements of the passed array, and then uses the DIV User-Defined Function to divide the sum by the number of elements in the array. This results in the average.

COMPUTING VARIANCE IN ARRAYS

The problem:

> You have a client who is working with arrays and statistics all the time, and who needs a series of functions to operate on these arrays. First, you have to sum all the elements in the array. Next, you need to compute the array's average. Now you have to compute the variance of the elements in an array.

The solution:

> Use a Procedure to compute the variance of the elements of an array.

The calling code:

```
*   . . .
    SET COLOR TO &ColStand
    CLEAR
    SET DECIMALS TO 6
    PUBLIC ARRAY ArrayN[10]
    ArrayN[1]   = 87
    ArrayN[2]   = 79
    ArrayN[3]   = 97
    ArrayN[4]   = 83
    ArrayN[5]   = 90
    ArrayN[6]   = 85
    ArrayN[7]   = 51
    ArrayN[8]   = 98
    ArrayN[9]   = 99
    ArrayN[10]  = 88
    TheVar      = 0
    DO AVAR WITH "ArrayN", 10, TheVar
    ? TheVar PICTURE 99,999.999999
*   The Variance of the array  =  193.122222
*   . . .
```

The Procedure:

```
PROCEDURE AVAR
*
*    Program...: AVAR
*    Author....: Phil Steele - President
*              Phillipps Computer Systems Inc.
*    Address...: 52 Hook Mountain Road,
*              Montville NJ 07045
*    Phone.....: (201) 575-8575
*    Date......: 01/02/89
*    Notice....: Copyright 1989  Philip Steele,
*              All Rights Reserved.
*    Notes.....: This function computes the variance of
*              the elements of an array
*    Parameters: AName - The name of an array
*                      containing numeric elements to
*                      obtain the variance of. The
*                      array must be declared public.
*              J     - The number of elements to
*                      be used for the variance.
*              Var   - The variance.
*
PARAMETERS AName, J, Var
PRIVATE N, Tot, SSq, Avg, Var, AName
STORE 0 TO Tot, SSq, Avg, Var
N = 1
DO WHILE N <= J
   Tot = Tot + &AName[N]
   SSq = SSq + (&AName[N] * &AName[N])
   N   = N   + 1
ENDDO
Var = (SSq - (Tot * Tot) / J) / (J - 1)
RETURN
*END:AVAR
```

Comments:

This UDF uses a DO WHILE loop to sum the elements of the passed array and compute the sum of squares of these elements. Then the variance is computed.

STANDARD DEVIATION OF ARRAYS

The problem:

> You have a client who is working with arrays and statistics all the time, and who needs a series of functions to operate on these arrays. First you have to sum all the elements in the array, then you need to compute the array's average and variance. Now you have to compute the standard deviation of the elements in an array.

The solution:

> Use a general-purpose User-Defined Function to compute the standard deviation of the elements of an array.

The calling code:

```
*  . . .
    SET COLOR TO &ColStand
    CLEAR
    SET DECIMALS TO 6
    PUBLIC ARRAY ArrayN[10]
    ArrayN[1]   = 87
    ArrayN[2]   = 79
    ArrayN[3]   = 97
    ArrayN[4]   = 83
    ArrayN[5]   = 90
    ArrayN[6]   = 85
    ArrayN[7]   = 51
    ArrayN[8]   = 98
    ArrayN[9]   = 99
    ArrayN[10]  = 88
    TheSD       = 0
    DO ASD WITH "ArrayN", 10, TheSD
    ? TheSD PICTURE "999.999999"
  * The Std Dev of the array  =  13.896842
  *  . . .
```

The Procedure:

```
PROCEDURE ASD
*
*   Program...: ASD
*   Author....: Phil Steele - President
*             Phillipps Computer Systems Inc.
*   Address...: 52 Hook Mountain Road,
*             Montville NJ 07045
*   Phone.....: (201) 575-8575
*   Date......: 01/02/89
*   Notice....: Copyright 1989  Philip Steele,
*             All Rights Reserved.
*   Notes.....: This function computes the standard
*             deviation of the elements of an array.
*   Parameters: AName - The name of an array
*                     containing numeric elements to
*                     obtain the Std Dev of. The
*                     array must be declared public.
*             J     - The number of elements to
*                     be used for the standard Dev.
*             Std   - The Standard Deviation.
*
PARAMETERS AName, J, Std
PRIVATE J, N, Tot, SSq, Avg, Var, Std, AName
* Note: If you already have a variance function
* just use the next two lines without the comments.
* DO AVar WITH "&AName", J, Var
* Std =  Var^0.5
STORE 0 TO Tot, SSq, Avg, Var, Std
N = 1
DO WHILE N <= J
   Tot = Tot + &AName[N]
   SSq = SSq + (&AName[N] * &AName[N])
   N   = N   + 1
ENDDO
Var = (SSq - (Tot * Tot) / J) / (J - 1)
Std = Var ^ 0.5
RETURN
*END:ASD
```

Comments:

This UDF uses a DO WHILE loop to sum the elements of the passed array, and compute the sum of squares of these elements. Then the variance and standard deviation are computed.

LOWEST VALUE IN ARRAYS

The problem:

> I had a client who was working with arrays all the time, and who needed a series of functions that operated on these arrays. After we had the function to compute the standard deviation of the elements in an array, we needed to find the element with the lowest value in the array.

The solution:

> I used a general-purpose User-Defined Function to find the element with the lowest value in the array.

The calling code:

```
*  . . .
   SET COLOR TO &ColStand
   CLEAR
   PUBLIC ARRAY ArrayN[9]
   ArrayN[1]  =  "ABC"
   ArrayN[2]  =  "AVD"
   ArrayN[3]  =  "VEF"
   ArrayN[4]  =  "BER"
   ArrayN[5]  =  "AAA"
   ArrayN[6]  =  "XEW"
   ArrayN[7]  =  "EWW"
   ArrayN[8]  =  "A"
   ArrayN[9]  =  "BBG"
   First  =  AMin(9)
   @ 20,5 SAY "The minimum value in the array is:" ;
                + First
*  The minimum value in the array is: A
*   . . .
```

The User-Defined Function:

```
FUNCTION AMIN
*┌────────────────────────────────────────────────────┐
*│ Program...: AMIN                                    │
*│ Author....: Phil Steele - President                 │
*│            Phillipps Computer Systems Inc.          │
*│ Address...: 52 Hook Mountain Road,                  │
*│            Montville NJ 07045                       │
*│ Phone.....: (201) 575-8575                          │
*│ Date......: 01/02/89                                │
*│ Notice....: Copyright 1989  Philip Steele,          │
*│            All Rights Reserved.                     │
*│ Notes.....: This function finds the element of the  │
*│            array containing the lowest value, and   │
*│            returns its value.                       │
*│ Parameters: NSize - Size of the array.              │
*│ Note:.....: The array which contains the elements   │
*│            containing the minimum value must be     │
*│            declared PUBLIC.                          │
*└────────────────────────────────────────────────────┘
PARAMETERS NSize
PRIVATE NSize, X, J
X = ArrayN[1]
J = 2
DO WHILE J <= NSize
   X = IIF(ArrayN[J]<X, ArrayN[J], X)
   J = J + 1
ENDDO
RETURN(X)
*END:AMIN
```

Comments:

This UDF uses a DO WHILE loop to find the element with the lowest value. It compares each element with the preceding element, and saves the lowest for the next comparison.

HIGHEST VALUE IN ARRAYS
The problem:

I had a client who was working with arrays all the time, and who needed a series of functions that operated on these arrays. After we had the function to compute the standard deviation of the elements in an array, we needed to find the element with the highest value in the array.

The solution:

I used a general-purpose User-Defined Function to find the element with the highest value in the array.

The calling code:

```
SET COLOR TO &ColStand
CLEAR
PUBLIC ARRAY ArrayN[9]
ArrayN[1]  =  "ABC"
ArrayN[2]  =  "AVD"
ArrayN[3]  =  "VEF"
ArrayN[4]  =  "BER"
ArrayN[5]  =  "AAA"
ArrayN[6]  =  "XEW"
ArrayN[7]  =  "EWW"
ArrayN[8]  =  "A"
ArrayN[9]  =  "BBG"
Last       =    AMax(9)
@ 20,5 SAY "The maximum value in the array is:" ;
            + Last
* The maximum value in the array is: XEW
*  . . .
```

The User-Defined Function:

```
FUNCTION AMAX
*
*|  Program...: AMAX
*|  Author....: Phil Steele - President
*|              Phillipps Computer Systems Inc.
*|  Address...: 52 Hook Mountain Road,
*|              Montville NJ 07045
*|  Phone.....: (201) 575-8575
*|  Date......: 01/02/89
*|  Notice....: Copyright 1989  Philip Steele,
*|              All Rights Reserved.
*|  Notes.....: This function finds the element of the
*|              array containing the highest value,
*|              and returns its value.
*|  Parameters: NSize - Size of the array.
*|  Note:.....: The array which contains the elements
*|              containing the maximum value must be
*|              declared PUBLIC.
*
PARAMETERS NSize
PRIVATE NSize, X, J
X = ArrayN[1]
J = 2
DO WHILE J <= NSize
    X = IIF(ArrayN[J]>X, ArrayN[J], X)
    J = J + 1
ENDDO
RETURN(X)
*END:AMAX
```

Comments:

This UDF uses a DO WHILE loop to find the element with the lowest value. It compares each element with the preceding element, and saves the lowest for the next comparison.

LISTING dBASE IV FILES
The problem:

> You have to present a list of available dBASE IV DBF files so that the user can choose those he wishes to write to floppy disk. You would like use an array for this application.

> You need to place the result of a DIR command into an array. Required is a mask, as input, which contains a valid extension such as PRG ,DOC, DBF or MEM. This extension must be usable for a DIR command. An extension of ??X or * is not valid.

The solution:

> Develop a Procedure to satisfy these specifications.

The calling code:

```
*  . . .
   SET COLOR TO &ColStand
   CLEAR
   OldName   =  "C:\DBASE\SAMPLES\Employee"
   FindThem  =  "*.PRG"
   @ 12,30 SAY "P R O C E S S I N G"
   DO MakeADir WITH OldName, FindThem
   ?ADIR[1]
   ?ADIR[2]
   ?ADIR[3]
*  . . .
```

The Procedure:

```
PROCEDURE MAKEADIR
*
*   Program...: MAKEADIR
*   Author....: Phil Steele - President
*              Phillipps Computer Systems Inc.
*   Address...: 52 Hook Mountain Road,
*              Montville NJ 07045
*   Phone.....: (201) 575-8575
*   Date......: 01/02/89
*   Notice....: Copyright 1989  Philip Steele,
*              All Rights Reserved.
*   Notes.....: This function returns an Array Filled
*              with directory entries based upon a
*              normal DOS mask.
*   Parameters: OldN  - The name of any existing DBF
*                       file.
*              Mask  - A DOS mask containing the DIR
*                       information required:Eg. *.PRG
*
*   Note:      ADir will be a PUBLIC array which
*              contains the directory data after this
*              UDF is run.
*
PARAMETERS OldN, Mask
PRIVATE    OldN, Mask
NewName  = "ADIR"
PUBLIC ARRAY FName[2]
PUBLIC ARRAY FType[2]
PUBLIC ARRAY FLen [2]
PUBLIC ARRAY FDec [2]
FName [1] = "FName"
FName [2] = "Ext"
FType [1] = "C"
FType [2] = "C"
FLen  [1] = 9
FLen  [2] = 3
FDec  [1] = 0
FDec  [2] = 0
DO MakeF WITH OldN, NewName, 2
RUN DIR &Mask >ADIR.TXT
USE ADIR
APPEND FROM ADIR.TXT SDF
GOTO TOP
DELETE ALL FOR Ext <> RIGHT(Mask,3)
PACK
GOTO TOP
PUBLIC ARRAY ADIR[RECCOUNT()]
J = 1
DO WHILE .NOT. EOF()
   ADIR[J] = TRIM(FName) + "." + LTRIM(Ext)
   J = J + 1
   SKIP
ENDDO
RUN DEL ADIR.DBF >NUL
RUN DEL ADIR.TXT >NUL
RETURN
*END:MAKEADIR
```

Comments:

This Procedure issues a DOS DIR command, and redirects its output to a file. It then uses the MAKEF Procedure described in the miscellaneous section of this book to create a temporary file to hold the results of the redirected DIR command in DBF format. It deletes non-valid data and places the resulting records into a PUBLIC array. Before returning to the calling procedure, it deletes all the temporary files it created.

SOMETHING LIKE *ACHOICE*

The problem:

> You have Clipper code which needs to be converted to dBASE IV. One of the functions provided by Clipper is "ACHOICE" which uses the elements of an array as bars in a menu.

The solution:

> Develop a Procedure to mimic Clipper's ACHOICE Function.

The calling code:

```
*  . . .
   SET COLOR TO &ColStand
   CLEAR
   PUBLIC ARRAY AMenu[5]
   AMenu[1]  =  "View Records"
   AMenu[2]  =  "Add a Record"
   AMenu[3]  =  "Delete a Record"
   AMenu[4]  =  "Change a Record"
   AMenu[5]  =  "Return to DOS"
   Choice  = 5
   DO ACHOICE WITH Choice
   @ 20,30 SAY "Your Choice is: "  + STR(Choice,1,0)
*  . . .
```

The Procedure:

```
PROCEDURE ACHOICE
*
*│ Program...: ACHOICE
*│ Author....: Phil Steele - President
*│            Phillipps Computer Systems Inc.
*│ Address...: 52 Hook Mountain Road,
*│            Montville NJ 07045
*│ Phone.....: (201) 575-8575
*│ Date......: 01/02/89
*│ Notice....: Copyright 1989  Philip Steele,
*│            All Rights Reserved.
*│ Notes.....: This function returns the user's choice
*│            where the PUBLIC array AMenu acts as
*│            individual bars in a menu.
*│ Parameters: Choice - Contains the number of prompts
*│                      in the array and returns the
*│                      user's selection.
*│            AMenu  - Must be a PUBLIC array which
*│                     contains "menu" choices.
*│
*│ Note......: All the values must be the same length
*│            fill with blanks if necessary.
*│
*│            MAXIMUM length  = 78 characters.
*│            MAXIMUM Entries = 20.
*
PARAMETERS Choice
PRIVATE X, Y, T, L, B, R, N
X  = AMenu[1]
LX = LEN(X)
T  = INT(((24 - Choice) / 2) - 1)
B  = T + Choice + 1
L  = INT((80 - LX) / 2)
R  = L + LX + 3
SET COLOR TO &ColMenu
@ T, L CLEAR TO B, R
@ T, L        TO B, R DOUBLE
DEFINE MENU Choose
N = 1
DO WHILE N <= Choice
   X = AMenu[N]
   Y = "Y" + STR(N,1,0)
   DEFINE PAD &Y OF Choose PROMPT X AT T+N, L+1
   N = N + 1
   ON SELECTION PAD &Y OF Choose DO ChooseIt WITH Choice
ENDDO
ACTIVATE MENU Choose
RETURN
*END:ACHOICE

PROCEDURE CHOOSEIT
PARAMETERS Choice
Choice = VAL(SUBSTR(PAD(),2,1))
DEACTIVATE MENU
RELEASE    MENU
DEACTIVATE WINDOW &WName
RELEASE    WINDOW &WName
RETURN
*END:CHOOSEIT
```

Comments:

This Procedure computes the size of the double box to draw around the array selections by using the size of the array, and the length of an element in the array. It draws a box on the screen, and places each element of the array into the box using the DEFINE PAD command in a unique manner. Look at the code:

```
X  =  AMenu[N]
Y  =  "Y"  +  STR(N,1,0)
DEFINE PAD &Y OF Choose . . .
```

First, equate the local variable "X" with an element in the array AMenu. Next, define the local variable "Y" as equal to the letter "Y" concatenated with the element number "N", of array AMenu. Finally, use the macro &Y in the DEFINE PAD command. For element 3, of array AMenu, the line would be interpreted as:

```
DEFINE PAD Y3 OF Choose PROMPT;
"Delete a Record" AT T + 3, L + 1
```

It then uses the ON SELECTION command which executes the procedure "CHOICE". The user's selection is returned to the calling procedure, and the menu is deactivated and released.

COPYING A RANGE OF ELEMENTS

The problem:

You have an application that requires copying a range of elements from one array to another.

The solution:

Develop a Procedure to copy elements from one array to another.

The calling code:

```
*  . . .
   SET COLOR TO &ColStand
   CLEAR
   PUBLIC ARRAY A[5], B[4]
   A[1]  =  "AAAAAAAAA"
   A[2]  =  "BBBBBBBBB"
   A[3]  =  "CCCCCCCCC"
   A[4]  =  "DDDDDDDDD"
   A[5]  =  "EEEEEEEEE"
   B[1]  =  "X"
   B[2]  =  "X"
   B[3]  =  "X"
   B[4]  =  "X"
   DO ACOPY WITH "A", "B", 2, 3, 1
        ? B[1]
        ? B[2]
        ? B[3]
        ? B[4]
*  The results should be:"
*  "BBBBBBBBB"
*  "CCCCCCCCC"
*  "DDDDDDDDD"
*  "X"
*  . . .
```

The Procedure:

```
PROCEDURE ACOPY
*
*  Program...: ACOPY
*  Author....: Phil Steele - President
*            Phillipps Computer Systems Inc.
*  Address...: 52 Hook Mountain Road,
*            Montville NJ 07045
*  Phone.....: (201) 575-8575
*  Date......: 01/02/89
*  Notice....: Copyright 1989  Philip Steele,
*            All Rights Reserved.
*  Notes.....: This function copies one array to
*            another.
*  Parameters: Array1 -  The source array (PUBLIC).
*            Array2 -  The target array (PUBLIC).
*            Start1 -  The starting element in the
*                      source array.
*            Numb   -  The number of elements to
*                      to copy.
*            Start2 -  The starting element in the
*                      target array.
*
PARAMETERS Array1, Array2, Start1, Numb, Start2
PRIVATE    Array1, Array2, Start1, Numb, Start2, N
N    = Start1
Numb = Numb + Start1 - 1
DO WHILE N <= Numb
   &Array2[Start2] = &Array1[Start1]
   Start1 = Start1 + 1
   Start2 = Start2 + 1
   N      = N       + 1
ENDDO
RETURN
*END:ACOPY
```

Comments:

This Procedure uses the passed values of the number of
elements, and the starting point, to set up a DO WHILE
loop that performs the copy.

SOMETHING LIKE *ADEL*

The problem:

> You have an application that requires deleting an element from the middle of an array in the same manner as Clipper's ADEL function.

The solution:

> Develop a Procedure to mimic Clipper's ADEL User-Defined Function.

The calling code:

```
*    . . .
SET COLOR TO &ColStand
CLEAR
PUBLIC ARRAY A[5]
A[1]  =  "AAAAAAAAA"
A[2]  =  "BBBBBBBBB"
A[3]  =  "CCCCCCCCC"
A[4]  =  "DDDDDDDDD"
A[5]  =  "EEEEEEEEE"
DO ADEL WITH "A", 5, 2
? A[1]
? A[2]
? A[3]
? A[4]
? A[5]
*    . . .
```

The Procedure:

```
PROCEDURE ADEL
*┌──────────────────────────────────────────────────┐
*│ Program...: ADEL                                   │
*│ Author....: Phil Steele - President                │
*│             Phillipps Computer Systems Inc.        │
*│ Address...: 52 Hook Mountain Road,                 │
*│             Montville NJ 07045                     │
*│ Phone.....: (201) 575-8575                         │
*│ Date......: 01/02/89                               │
*│ Notice....: Copyright 1989  Philip Steele,         │
*│             All Rights Reserved.                   │
*│ Notes.....: This function deletes an element of    │
*│             an array.                              │
*│ Parameters: Array -  The name of the array to      │
*│                      delete an element from.       │
*│             Size  -  The number of elements in the │
*│                      array.                        │
*│             Numb  -  The number of element to be   │
*│                      deleted                       │
*│ Note: The contents of the deleted element is lost  │
*│       and all other elements are shifted up one.   │
*│       The last position of the array is undefined. │
*└──────────────────────────────────────────────────┘
PARAMETERS Array, Size, Numb
PRIVATE    Array, Size, Numb, N
DO WHILE Numb < Size
   &Array[Numb] = &Array[Numb+1]
   Numb = Numb + 1
ENDDO
&Array[Size] = .F.
RETURN
*END:ADEL
```

Comments:

This Procedure deletes the requested element by setting it equal to the next element in the array. This process is repeated until all the elements have been moved up one position, starting with the element to be deleted. The last element in the array is then set to FALSE.

SOMETHING LIKE *AINS*

The problem:

You have an application that requires inserting an element from the middle of an array, in the same manner as Clipper's AINS function.

The solution:

Develop a Procedure to mimic Clipper's AINS User-Defined Function.

The calling code:

```
*   . . .
SET COLOR TO &ColStand
CLEAR
PUBLIC ARRAY A[5]
A[1]  =  "AAAAAAAAA"
A[2]  =  "BBBBBBBBB"
A[3]  =  "CCCCCCCCC"
A[4]  =  "DDDDDDDDD"
A[5]  =  "EEEEEEEEE"
DO AINS WITH "A", 5, 2
? A[1]
? A[2]
? A[3]
? A[4]
? A[5]
*   . . .
```

The Procedure:

```
PROCEDURE AINS
*
*| Program...: AINS
*| Author....: Phil Steele - President
*|             Phillipps Computer Systems Inc.
*| Address...: 52 Hook Mountain Road,
*|             Montville NJ 07045
*| Phone.....: (201) 575-8575
*| Date......: 01/02/89
*| Notice....: Copyright 1989  Philip Steele,
*|             All Rights Reserved.
*| Notes.....: This function inserts an element into
*|             an array.
*| Parameters: Array -  The name of the array to
*|                      insert an element into.
*|             Size  -  The number of elements in the
*|                      array.
*|             Numb  -  The number of element to be
*|                      inserted.
*| Note: The contents of the inserted element is
*|       undefined and all other elements are shifted
*|       down one position and the last array element
*|       is lost.
*
PARAMETERS Array, Size, Numb
PRIVATE    Array, Size, Numb, N
DO WHILE Size > Numb
   &Array[Size] = &Array[Size-1]
   Size = Size - 1
ENDDO
&Array[Numb] = .F.
RETURN
*END:AINS
```

Comments:

This Procedure inserts the requested element into the array, and sets it equal to FALSE. Each element after the inserted element, is moved down one position by setting it equal to the previous element in the array. This process is repeated until all the elements have been moved down one position, starting with the element to be inserted. The last element in the array is lost using this procedure.

ARRAY FILL

The problem:

You have an application that requires filling an array
with a string, starting at a specified point, for a specified
number of elements.

The solution:

Develop a Procedure to fill an array with a constant.

The calling code:

```
*  . . .
SET COLOR TO &ColStand
CLEAR
PUBLIC ARRAY A[5]
DO AFILL WITH "A", "ABCDEFG", 2, 3
? A[1]
? A[2]
? A[3]
? A[4]
? A[5]
*. . .
```

The Procedure:

```
PROCEDURE AFILL
*
* | Program...: AFILL
* | Author....: Phil Steele - President
* |             Phillipps Computer Systems Inc.
* | Address...: 52 Hook Mountain Road,
* |             Montville NJ 07045
* | Phone.....: (201) 575-8575
* | Date......: 01/02/89
* | Notice....: Copyright 1989  Philip Steele,
* |             All Rights Reserved.
* | Notes.....: This function an array with the value
* |             of an element.
* | Parameters: Array - The name of the array to
* |                     fill with a value.
* |             Exp   - The expression to fill the
* |                     array with.
* |             Start - The number of the element to
* |                     start with.
* |             Size  - The number of elements to Fill
*
PARAMETERS Array, Exp, Start, Size
PRIVATE    Array, Exp, Start, Size, N
N = 1
DO WHILE N <= Size
   &Array[Start] = Exp
   Start = Start + 1
   N     = N + 1
ENDDO
RETURN
*END:AFILL
```

Comments:

This Procedure fills an array with the value contained in the passed variable "Exp". It starts with the passed element "Start" and continues until the element "Size" is reached.

FINDING A RANGE

The problem:

You have to find the element in an array that contains a string. However, you only want to look at elements in the array greater than 5 and less than 30. The value to be returned is the element number of the array containing the string. If the string is not found, a zero must be returned.

The solution:

Develop a Procedure to find a specific element in an array.

The calling code:

```
*    . . .
SET COLOR TO &ColStand
CLEAR
PUBLIC ARRAY A[5]
A[1]  =  "ABCDEF"
A[2]  =  "GHIJKL"
A[3]  =  "MNOPQR"
A[4]  =  "MNOPQR"
A[5]  =  "MNOPQR"
X     = 7
DO ASCAN WITH "A" "OPQ", 1, 3, X
? X           && ANSWER  =  3
X = 7
DO ASCAN WITH "A," "PQR", 4, 2, X
? X           && ANSWER  =  4
X = 7
DO ASCAN WITH "A", "WXY", 1, 5, X
? X           && ANSWER  =  0
*  . . .
```

The Procedure:

```
PROCEDURE ASCAN
*┌──────────────────────────────────────────────────────┐
*│ Program...: ASCAN                                      │
*│ Author....: Phil Steele - President                    │
*│             Phillipps Computer Systems Inc.            │
*│ Address...: 52 Hook Mountain Road,                     │
*│             Montville NJ 07045                         │
*│ Phone.....: (201) 575-8575                             │
*│ Date......: 01/02/89                                   │
*│ Notice....: Copyright 1989  Philip Steele,             │
*│             All Rights Reserved.                       │
*│ Notes.....: This function scans an array for a         │
*│             specific string value.                     │
*│ Parameters: Array -  The name of the array to          │
*│                      scan.                             │
*│             Exp   -  The expression to scan for.       │
*│             Start -  The number of the element to      │
*│                      start with.                       │
*│             Size  -  The number of elements to scan    │
*│             Ret   -  The element position of first     │
*│                      matching value - 0 if no match    │
*│                      is found.                         │
*└──────────────────────────────────────────────────────┘
*
PARAMETERS Array, Exp, Start, Size, Ret
PRIVATE    Array, Exp, Start, Size, N, Z, K, LExp, LA,;
           MLen, Y
LExp = LEN(Exp)
N    = 1
Ret  = 0
DO WHILE N <= Size
   Z    = &Array[Start]
   K    = 1
   LA   = LEN(Z)
   MLen = LA - LExp + 1
   DO WHILE K <= MLen
      Y = SUBSTR(Z, K, LExp)
      IF Y = Exp
         Ret = Start
         EXIT
      ENDIF
      K = K + 1
   ENDDO
   IF Ret = 0
      Start = Start + 1
      N     = N + 1
   ELSE
      EXIT
   ENDIF
ENDDO
RETURN
*END:ASCAN
```

Comments:

This Procedure tries to find an element in the array "Array" containing the value in "Exp". It starts the search at element number "Start" and continues until the element "Size" is reached. If the substring is found in a valid array element, the number of that element is returned—otherwise, a zero is returned.

SORTING AN ARRAY

The problem:

> You have to sort an array prior to displaying the elements.

The solution:

> Develop a Procedure to sort an array.

The calling code:

```
*  . . .
   SET COLOR TO &ColStand
   CLEAR
   PUBLIC ARRAY SArray[9]
   SArray[1]  =  "PHIL"
   SArray[2]  =  "Phil"
   SArray[3]  =  "PHILL"
   SArray[4]  =  "phill"
   SArray[5]  =  "Philip"
   SArray[6]  =  "ALAN"
   SArray[7]  =  "JOHN"
   SArray[8]  =  "      "
   SArray[9]  =  "Phillip"
   NumOfElem  =  9
   J  =  1
   ? "Pre-Sort"
   DO WHILE J < =  NumOfElem
        ? SArray[J]
        J  =  J + 1
   ENDDO
   DO ASORT WITH "SArray",NumOfElem
   J  =  1
   ? " "
   ? "Post-Sort"
   DO WHILE J < =  NumOfElem
        ? SArray[J]
        J  =  J + 1
   ENDDO
*  . . .
```

The Procedure:

```
PROCEDURE ASORT
*
*|  Program...: ASORT
*|  Author....: Phil Steele - President
*|             Phillipps Computer Systems Inc.
*|  Address...: 52 Hook Mountain Road,
*|             Montville NJ 07045
*|  Phone.....: (201) 575-8575
*|  Date......: 01/02/89
*|  Notice....: Copyright 1989  Philip Steele,
*|             All Rights Reserved.
*|  Notes.....: This function sorts an array ascending.
*|  Parameters: AName - The array to sort.
*|              ALen  - The number of array elements.
*
PARAMETERS AName, ALen
PRIVATE J, K, C, ALen, AName
J = 1
DO WHILE J <= ALen - 1
   K = J + 1
   DO WHILE K <=  ALen
      IF &AName[K] < &AName[J]
         C           = &AName[K]
         &AName[K] = &AName[J]
         &AName[J] = C
      ENDIF
      K = K + 1
   ENDDO
   J = J + 1
ENDDO
RETURN
*END:ASORT
```

Comments:

This Procedure uses a bubble sort to sort the elements in an array.

5

Business Functions

I had a client who needed to duplicate the business functions available in a spreadsheet language in his Clipper application.

Because I use business and financial terms in this section with which some readers may not be familiar, I will now define them.

PERIODIC INTEREST RATE—This is the amount of interest paid or received over a period of time. This figure is usually annualized. If you borrow $120 for one year, and agree to repay the lender $132 at the end of the year, the cost of borrowing is $12, and this is considered a SIMPLE INTEREST LOAN. The *periodic interest rate* is $12/$120 or 10% per year. If this transaction was for a month instead of a year, the calculation is still $12/$120 or 10%, but the term is now one month. The periodic interest rate is 10% per month or 120% per year!

TAX-FREE BOND—A *bond* is a long-term promissory note issued by a corporation or municipality when it borrows funds. Normally, the lender must pay taxes on the interest received from the borrower. However, in the case of municipalities, no federal or state tax is due on this interest. In this case you have a *tax-free bond*. Note: a recent Supreme Court decision makes it possible for the federal government to change the laws regarding the tax-free status of municipal bonds.

COMPOUNDED MONTHLY—Interest can be compounded over various time periods. Let's use an example to explain compound interest. You just purchased a computer program for $200. The vendor allowed you to pay over one year with only 1% per month interest charge on the outstanding balance. At the end of the first month, you would owe $200 * 1.01 or $202. If you did not pay anything at the end of the month, you would owe $202 * 1.01 or $204.02 at the end of two months. At the end of 12 months you would owe $(1.01)^{12}$ * $200 or $225.36. In short, *compounded interest* is nothing more than interest on interest.

COMPOUNDING PERIODS—Interest can be compounded over various time periods, such as daily, monthly, annually, etc. The period used to compute the interest is called the *compounding period*.

FIXED INTEREST RATE—This is the rate of interest that is fixed over a period of time. If you received 10% per year over the life of your investment, you would be getting a *fixed interest rate* of 10% annually.

FIXED PAYMENTS—When you obtain a loan, you usually repay the same amount on a periodic basis. For example you borrow $120 for a year, and pay back $11.00 per month—this is a *fixed payment*. If you buy $100 worth of IBM stock each month, you are buying stock with a fixed payment investment. When the price of the stock is low, you buy more shares for your $100 than when the price is high.

IRA ACCOUNT—An IRA (Individual Retirement Account) is a special account containing tax deferred deposits and interest. An individual with earned income is permitted to set aside up to

$2,000.00 per year, depending upon income. The amount set aside can be deducted from the taxpayer's income, and will be subject to income tax only upon withdrawal.

Note: There has been a recent change in the IRS code which affects the qualifying limits for Individual Retirement Accounts.

TERM OF AN INVESTMENT—The *term of an investment* is the amount of time it takes a periodic dollar amount to grow to a predetermined value, when invested at a given rate of return— for example, if you put $2,000 per year in the bank and received 9.5% per year interest. You want to know how many years it will take to accumulate $200,000, the term of the investment. In this case the term of the investment would be 25 years and 11 months. The $2,000 deposited each year is considered to be a PERIODIC INVESTMENT.

AMOUNT OF A LOAN PAYMENT—At times, you want to know how much a loan will cost you per time period: the amount of a loan. You know that you can obtain $250,000 for 30 years at 11.5%, but how much do you have to pay back per month? What is the amount of a loan payment? This calculation is usually performed when computing a FIXED-RATE MORTGAGE. A fixed-rate mortgage is nothing more than a loan with an interest rate that doesn't vary over the life of the loan. The previous example could be considered a 30-year, fixed-rate mortgage if a lien on specific property was given by the borrower as security for the loan.

DEPRECIATION—Depreciation is a deduction of part of the cost of an asset from income in each year of the asset's life. For example, I buy a PS/2 model 80 computer for $8,000. Because the life of the computer is longer than one year, I can't deduct the entire $8,000 in one year, so I deduct a portion of the $8,000 each year over the computer's life. This deduction is the depreciation. Different methods or techniques can be used to compute the depreciation.

DOUBLE-DECLINING BALANCE METHOD—This is a technique of computing depreciation used to provide a higher depreciation allowance in the early years of an asset's life. The formula used is:

DDB = 2 * (Current book value / Depreciable life)

If the life of the $8,000 PS/2 is four years, then the straight-line depreciation for year one would be $2,000, and the double-declining balance method depreciation would be $4,000.

SALVAGE VALUE—the price that can be received for an asset after it has been used for most of its useful life. I purchased an IBM PC for my business in 1982 for $4,000. After using it for five years, I could sell it for $800. Its salvage value is $800.

PERIODIC INTEREST RATE

The problem:

You purchased a tax-free bond for $10,000 that matures in 12 years, pays $27,000 when it matures, and interest is compounded monthly. What interest rate is it earning?

The solution:

Create a User-Defined Function to compute the interest rate.

The calling code:

```
*    . . .
     SET COLOR TO &ColStand
     CLEAR
     Mat    = 27000
     Now    = 10000
     Yrs    = 12
     NRate  = Rate(Mat, Now, Yrs)
     ? NRate PICTURE "9.9999"
*    NRate Should be 0.0831 or 8.31%
*    . . .
```

The User-Defined Function:

```
FUNCTION RATE
*
*| Program...: RATE
*| Author....: Phil Steele - President
*|             Phillipps Computer Systems Inc.
*| Address...: 52 Hook Mountain Road,
*|             Montville NJ 07045
*| Phone.....: (201) 575-8575
*| Date......: 01/02/89
*| Notice....: Copyright 1989  Philip Steele,
*|             All Rights Reserved.
*| Notes.....: This function computes the interest
*|             rate an investments earns.
*| Parameters: Mat - The dollar amount the investment
*|                   is worth at maturity.
*|             Now - The dollar amount the investment
*|                   is worth at the start.
*|             Yrs - The number of years required for
*|                   the investment to go from a
*|                   starting value of Now to a final
*|                   value of Mat.
*
PARAMETERS Mat, Now, Yrs
PRIVATE N, D, M , R
M = Yrs * 12
N = Mat
D = Now
R = ((N / D) ^ (1 / M)) - 1
RETURN(R*12)
*END:RATE
```

Comments:

This UDF uses a standard formula to compute the interest rate of an investment.

$$Rate = ((fv/pv)^{1/n}) - 1.$$

$$Rate = ((Future\ value\ /\ present\ value)^{(1/term)}) - 1.$$

COMPOUNDING PERIODS TOWARD FUTURE VALUE

The problem:

You deposited $10,000 in an account that pays 10% per year (annual interest rate) compounded monthly. How long will it take for your $10,000 to double?

The solution:

Write a general-purpose User-Defined Function to compute the number of compounding periods it takes an investment to grow to some future value, earning a fixed interest rate per compounding period.

The calling code:

```
*    . . .
     SET COLOR TO &ColStand
     CLEAR
     Int    = 10
     Mat    = 20000
     Now    = 10000
     NMonth = Term(Int, Mat, Now)
     ? NMonth PICTURE "99.99"
*    NMonth Should be 83.52
*    . . .
```

The User-Defined Function:

```
FUNCTION TERM
*
*   Program...: TERM
*   Author....: Phil Steele - President
*             Phillipps Computer Systems Inc.
*   Address...: 52 Hook Mountain Road,
*             Montville NJ 07045
*   Phone.....: (201) 575-8575
*   Date......: 01/02/89
*   Notice....: Copyright 1989  Philip Steele,
*             All Rights Reserved.
*   Notes.....: This function computes the time
*             required for an investment to grow
*             from a value of Now to a value of Mat
*             at a compound interest rate of Int.
*   Parameters: Mat - The dollar amount the investment
*                 is worth at maturity.
*             Now - The dollar amount the investment
*                 is worth at the start.
*             Int - The compound interest rate which
*                 the investment in invested at.
*
PARAMETERS Int, Mat, Now
PRIVATE N, D, I
I = Int * 0.01 / 12
N = LOG(Mat / Now)
D = LOG(1 + I)
RETURN(N/D)
*END:TERM
```

Comments:

This UDF uses a standard formula to compute the term of an investment.

Term = ln(fv/pv) / ln(1 + in).

Term = Natural Log (future value / present value) /
(Natural Log(1 + Periodic interest rate)).

TIME FOR GROWTH

The problem:

You plan to deposit $2,000 a year in your IRA account. You can get 9.5% per year interest compounded annually. How many years will it take to have $200,000 in the account?

The solution:

Write a User-Defined Function to compute the number of fixed payments, earning a fixed interest rate per compounding period, that is needed to accumulate a fixed dollar amount.

The calling code:

```
*    . . .
     SET COLOR TO &ColStand
     CLEAR
         Int    = 9.5
         Mat    = 200000
         Dep    = 2000
         NYrs   = Term2(Dep, Int, Mat)
     ? NYrs PICTURE "99.99"
*    NYrs Should be 25.91
*    . . .
```

The User-Defined Function:

```
FUNCTION TERM2
*
*  Program...: TERM2
*  Author....: Phil Steele - President
*             Phillipps Computer Systems Inc.
*  Address...: 52 Hook Mountain Road,
*             Montville NJ 07045
*  Phone.....: (201) 575-8575
*  Date......: 01/02/89
*  Notice....: Copyright 1989  Philip Steele,
*             All Rights Reserved.
*  Notes.....: This function computes the time
*             required for a periodic investment
*             to grow to a value of Mat at a
*             compound interest rate of Int.
*  Parameters: Mat - The dollar amount the investment
*                    is worth at maturity.
*             Dep - The dollar amount of the
*                    periodic investment.
*             Int - The compound interest rate which
*                    the investment in invested at.
*
PARAMETERS Dep, Int, Mat
PRIVATE N, D
IR = Int * 0.01
N  = LOG(1 + (Mat * IR / Dep))
D  = LOG(1 + IR)
RETURN(N/D)
*END:TERM2
```

Comments:

This UDF uses a standard formula to compute the term of an investment.

Term $= \ln(1 + (\text{fv}*\text{in}/\text{pmt})) / \ln(1 + \text{int})$.

Term $=$ Natural $\log(1 +$ (future value $*$ periodic interest rate / periodic payment)) / Natural $\log(1 +$ periodic interest rate).

ANNUAL DEPRECIATION: METHOD ONE
The problem:

You just purchased an IBM PS/2 model 80 with all the bells and whistles for $10,000. You estimate that you could sell it for $2,000 in 5 years. How much depreciation can you take in year number two, using various depreciation methods?

The solution:

Use general-purpose User-Defined Functions to compute depreciation using different methods. The first of these is the straight-line method—where you take the same amount of depreciation every month based upon the cost of the asset and the salvage value.

The calling code:

```
*   . . .
    SET COLOR TO &ColStand
    CLEAR
        Cost        = 10000
        Sal         = 2000
        Life        = 5
        Yr          = 2
        SDep        = SL (Cost, Sal, Life)
    ? SDep PICTURE "9,999.99"      && $1,600.00
*   . . .
```

The User-Defined Function:

```
FUNCTION SL
*
*   Program...: SL
*   Author....: Phil Steele - President
*             Phillipps Computer Systems Inc.
*   Address...: 52 Hook Mountain Road,
*             Montville NJ 07045
*   Phone.....: (201) 575-8575
*   Date......: 01/02/89
*   Notice....: Copyright 1989  Philip Steele,
*             All Rights Reserved.
*   Notes.....: This function computes the annual
*             depreciation of an asset with salvage
*             value of Sal over a useful life of
*             Life.
*   Parameters: Cost - Cost of the asset.
*             Sal  - Salvage value of the asset.
*             Life - Useful life of the asset.
*
PARAMETERS C, S, L
PRIVATE     C, S
N = (C - S)
RETURN(N/L)
*END:SL
```

Comments:

This UDF uses a standard formula to compute the straight-line depreciation of the asset.

SLD = (C-S)/L.

Annual straight-line depreciation =
        (Cost - Salvage value) / Useful life.

ANNUAL DEPRECIATION: METHOD TWO

The problem:

You just purchased an IBM PS/2 model 80 with all the bells and whistles for $10,000. You estimate that you could sell it for $2,000 in 5 years. How much depreciation can you take in year number two, using various depreciation methods?

The solution:

Use general-purpose User-Defined Functions to compute depreciation using different methods. Another method is the sum-of-the-years'-digits method of depreciation, which is based upon the cost of the asset and the salvage value.

The calling code:

```
*    . . .
     SET COLOR TO &ColStand
     CLEAR
          Cost  = 10000
          Sal   = 2000
          Life  = 5
          Yr    = 2
          YDep  = SYD(Cost, Sal, Life, Yr)
     ? YDep PICTURE "9,999.99"      && $2,133.33
*    . . .
```

The User-Defined Function:

```
FUNCTION SYD
*┌──────────────────────────────────────────────────────┐
*│ Program...: SYD                                        │
*│ Author....: Phil Steele - President                    │
*│            Phillipps Computer Systems Inc.             │
*│ Address...: 52 Hook Mountain Road,                     │
*│            Montville NJ 07045                          │
*│ Phone.....: (201) 575-8575                             │
*│ Date......: 01/02/89                                   │
*│ Notice....: Copyright 1989  Philip Steele,             │
*│            All Rights Reserved.                        │
*│ Notes.....: This function computes the yearly (Yr)     │
*│            depreciation of an asset with salvage       │
*│            value of Sal over a useful life of          │
*│            Life.                                        │
*│ Parameters: Cost - Cost of the asset.                  │
*│            Sal  - Salvage value of the asset.          │
*│            Life - Useful life of the asset.            │
*│            Yr   - The year you wish to compute         │
*│                   the depreciation for.                │
*└──────────────────────────────────────────────────────┘
PARAMETERS C, S, L, Y
PRIVATE    C, S, L, Y
N = (C - S) * (L - Y + 1)
D = (L * (L + 1) / 2)
RETURN(N/D)
*END:SYD
```

Comments:

This UDF uses a standard formula to compute the sum-of-the-years'-digits method of depreciation of the asset.

$SYD = (C-S)*(L-Y+1) / (L*(L+1)/2)$.

Sum-of-the-years'-digits depreciation =
            (Cost - Salvage value) *
        (Useful life - Number of years to depreciate + 1) /
            (Useful life * (Useful life + 1) / 2).

ANNUAL DEPRECIATION: METHOD THREE

The problem:

You just purchased an IBM PS/2 model 80 with all the bells and whistles for $10,000. You estimate that you could sell it for $2,000 in 5 years. How much depreciation can you take in year number two using various depreciation methods?

The solution:

Use general-purpose User-Defined Functions to compute depreciation using different methods. This example uses the double-declining method of depreciation, which is based upon the cost of the asset and the salvage value.

The calling code:

```
*   . . .
    SET COLOR TO &ColStand
    CLEAR
        Cost  =  10000
        Sal   =  2000
        Life  =  5
        Yr    =  2
        DDep  =  DDL(Cost, Sal, Life, Yr)
    ? DDep PICTURE "9,999.99"
*   DDep Should be $2,400.00
*   . . .
```

The User-Defined Function:

```
FUNCTION DDL
*
*   Program...: DDL
*   Author....: Phil Steele - President
*               Phillipps Computer Systems Inc.
*   Address...: 52 Hook Mountain Road,
*               Montville NJ 07045
*   Phone.....: (201) 575-8575
*   Date......: 01/02/89
*   Notice....: Copyright 1989  Philip Steele,
*               All Rights Reserved.
*   Notes.....: This function computes the yearly (Yr)
*               depreciation of an asset with salvage
*               value of Sal over a useful life of
*               Life.
*   Parameters: Cost - Cost of the asset.
*               Sal  - Salvage value of the asset.
*               Life - Useful life of the asset.
*               Yr   - The year you wish to compute
*                      the depreciation for.
*
PARAMETERS C, S, L, Y
PRIVATE    C, S, L, Y, N, NewTotal, TotDep
CLEAR
DECLARE YrDep[L]
NewTotal = C
TotDep   = 0
N        = 1
DO WHILE N <= Y
   YrDep[N] = NewTotal * 2 / L
   NewTotal = NewTotal - YrDep[N]
   TotDep   = IIF(N<=Y, TotDep+YrDep[N], TotDep)
   N = N + 1
ENDDO
RETURN(YrDep[Y])
*END:DDL
```

Comments:

This UDF uses a DO WHILE loop to compute the double-declining method of depreciation of the asset. It computes the depreciation each year, and places the results into an array. It then computes the total depreciation taken to date. Based upon these values, it computes the depreciation for the month required.

DATES AND WEEKENDS

The problem:

You are developing code for a large business system. No computations can take place on Saturday or Sunday. How do you know when a weekend occurs?

The solution:

Develop a general-purpose User-Defined Function to determine if a date falls on a weekend.

The calling code:

```
*   . . .
    SET COLOR TO &ColStand
    CLEAR
    X = {12/7/41}
    @ 11,12 SAY DTOC(X) + " is" + ;
        IIF(.NOT. ISWKEND(X), " not ", " ") + ;
        "a weekend."

    X = {12/25/41}
    @ 13,12 SAY DTOC(X) + " is" + ;
        IIF(.NOT. ISWKEND(X), " not ", " ") + ;
        "a weekend."
*   . . .
```

The User-Defined Function:

```
FUNCTION ISWKEND
*
* Program...: ISWKEND
* Author....: Phil Steele - President
*             Phillipps Computer Systems Inc.
* Address...: 52 Hook Mountain Road,
*             Montville NJ 07045
* Phone.....: (201) 575-8575
* Date......: 01/02/89
* Notice....: Copyright 1989  Philip Steele,
*             All Rights Reserved.
* Notes.....: This procedure returns A .T. if a date
*             occurs on a Saturday or Sunday.
* Parameters: WKDate - The date to check.
*
PARAMETERS WKDate
RETURN(IIF(DOW(WKDate)=1 .OR. DOW(WKDate)=7, .T., .F.))
*END:ISWKEND
```

Comments:

This UDF uses the built-in function DOW (day of week) to determine if the date is a Saturday or Sunday, and returns a TRUE if this is the case.

NUMBERS TO WORDS

The problem:

You have to print checks, and you need a method to convert a dollar amount to a word representation. For example: $1,010.50 must print as ONE THOUSAND TEN DOLLARS AND 50 CENTS.

The solution:

Develop a general-purpose User-Defined Function to convert a numeric dollar amount to a word dollar amount.

The calling code:

```
*   . . .
SET COLOR TO &ColStand
CLEAR
X  =  987654.32
Z  =  Checks(X)
? Z
X  =  100005.09
Z  =  Checks(X)
? Z
X  =  10005.15
Z  =  Checks(X)
? Z
X  =  1005.00
Z  =  Checks(X)
? Z
X  =  105.98
Z  =  Checks(X)
? Z
X  =  15.11
Z  =  Checks(X)
? Z
X  =  5.12
Z  =  Checks(X)
? Z
X  =  0.02
Z  =  Checks(X)
? Z
*   . . .
```

The User-Defined Function:

```
FUNCTION CHECKS
*
*   Program...: CHECKS
*   Author....: Phil Steele - President
*             Phillipps Computer Systems Inc.
*   Address...: 52 Hook Mountain Road,
*             Montville NJ 07045
*   Phone.....: (201) 575-8575
*   Date......: 01/02/89
*   Notice....: Copyright 1989  Philip Steele,
*             All Rights Reserved.
*   Notes.....: This function returns the passed
*             number as a dollar amount written out.
*   Parameters: Num - The number to be converted to a
*                 word.
*   Note......: This function ONLY works with numbers
*             numbers less than one million with a
*             decimal point and two digits to the
*             right. 999999.99 Maximum.
*
PARAMETERS Num
PRIVATE     NLen, HT, TT, TH, HU, TE, UN, SNum, Ret, X
SNum = LTRIM(STR(Num))
NLen = LEN(SNum)
SNum = REPLICATE("0",6-NLen) + SNum
HT   = SUBSTR(SNum, 1, 1)
TT   = SUBSTR(SNum, 2, 1)
TH   = SUBSTR(SNum, 3, 1)
HU   = SUBSTR(SNum, 4, 1)
TE   = SUBSTR(SNum, 5, 1)
UN   = SUBSTR(SNum, 6, 1)
Ret  = Hund(HT) + Teens(TT, TH) + Thou(TH, NLen) +;
       Hund(HU) + Teens(TE, UN) + Unit(UN, TE)
Ret  = IIF(LEN(TRIM(Ret))=0, " zero", Ret)
Ret  = Ret + " DOLLARS and"
SNum = LTRIM(STR(Num,20,2))
TE   = SUBSTR(SNum,AT(".",SNum)+1,1)
UN   = SUBSTR(SNum,AT(".",SNum)+2,1)
X    = Teens(TE, UN) + Unit(UN, TE)
X    = IIF(LEN(TRIM(X))=0, " zero", X)
Ret  = LTRIM(Ret + X + " CENTS")
RETURN(Ret)
*END:CHECKS

FUNCTION HUND
PARAMETERS H
PRIVATE     H, Ans
Ans = Unit(H, "6")
Ans = IIF(LEN(TRIM(Ans))=0, Ans, Ans+" hundred")
RETURN(Ans)
*END:HUND

FUNCTION THOU
PARAMETERS H, NLen
PRIVATE     H, Ans
```

```
Ans = Unit(H, "6")
Ans = IIF(NLen>3, Ans+" thousand", " ")
RETURN(Ans)
*END:THOU

FUNCTION TEENS
PARAMETERS T, U
PRIVATE     T, U, Ans
DO CASE
    CASE T = "1"
        DO CASE
            CASE U = "0"
                T = " ten"
            CASE U = "1"
                T = " eleven"
            CASE U = "2"
                T = " twelve"
            CASE U = "3"
                T = " thirteen"
            CASE U = "4"
                T = " fourteen"
            CASE U = "5"
                T = " fifteen"
            CASE U = "6"
                T = " sixteen"
            CASE U = "7"
                T = " seventeen"
            CASE U = "8"
                T = " eighteen"
            CASE U = "9"
                T = " nineteen"
        ENDCASE
    CASE T = "2"
        T = " twenty"
    CASE T = "3"
        T = " thirty"
    CASE T = "4"
        T = " forty"
    CASE T = "5"
        T = " fifty"
    CASE T = "6"
        T = " sixty"
    CASE T = "7"
        T = " seventy"
    CASE T = "8"
        T = " eighty"
    CASE T = "9"
        T = " ninety"
    CASE T = "0"
        T = ""
ENDCASE
Ans = T
RETURN(Ans)
*END:TEENS

FUNCTION UNIT
```

```
PARAMETERS X, Y
PRIVATE    X, Y
IF Y = "1"
   RETURN("")
ENDIF
DO CASE
   CASE X = "1"
      X = " one"
   CASE X = "2"
      X = " two"
   CASE X = "3"
      X = " three"
   CASE X = "4"
      X = " four"
   CASE X = "5"
      X = " five"
   CASE X = "6"
      X = " six"
   CASE X = "7"
      X = " seven"
   CASE X = "8"
      X = " eight"
   CASE X = "9"
      X = " nine"
   CASE X = "0"
      X = ""
ENDCASE
RETURN(X)
*END:UNIT
```

Comments:

This UDF parses the number, and then uses a series of
case statements to "translate" the parsed number into
words.

DISPLAYING DOLLAR AMOUNTS

The problem:

You have to display a dollar amount on the screen. The number can be between $10 and $10,000,000. When you try to print the number, you find that you can print either: $$$$$$$$$10 or $ 10, if you leave enough room for the ten million dollar figure. What are you going to do?

The solution:

Write a Procedure to print an integer with a floating dollar sign and commas.

The calling code:

```
*    . . .
SET COLOR TO &ColStand
CLEAR
X = 1234
Y = 1234567
Z = 12
@ 10,0 SAY "12345678901234567890"
@ 11,5 SAY X PICTURE "$999,999,999"
DO DFLOATI WITH 12, 5, 15, X
DO DFLOATI WITH 13, 5, 15, Y
DO DFLOATI WITH 14, 5, 15, Z
*    . . .
```

The Procedure:

```
PROCEDURE DFLOATI
*
*  Program...: DFLOATI
*  Author....: Phil Steele - President
*              Phillipps Computer Systems Inc.
*  Address...: 52 Hook Mountain Road,
*              Montville NJ 07045
*  Phone.....: (201) 575-8575
*  Date......: 01/02/89
*  Notice....: Copyright 1989  Philip Steele,
*              All Rights Reserved.
*  Notes.....: This procedure places a dollar sign
*              next to the high order digit of an
*              integer with no intervening spaces.
*              $1,234
*  Parameters: PRow - The row to print the number on.
*              PCol - The col where the high order
*                     digit of the largest number
*                     would print.
*              FLen - The length of the picture
*                     clause.
*              Num  - The number to print with a
*                     leading dollar sign.
*
PARAMETERS PRow, PCol, FLen, Num
PRIVATE    PRow, PCol, FLen, Num, NLen, NBlanks
NLen    = LEN(LTRIM(STR(Num,19,2)))
NBlanks = FLen - NLen - 1
DO CASE
   CASE NLen > 9
      NBlanks = NBlanks - 2
      Pic = "@B $" + REPLICATE("9",NLen-9) + ",999,999"
   CASE NLen > 6
      NBlanks = NBlanks - 1
      Pic = "@B $" + REPLICATE("9",NLen-6) + ",999"
   CASE NLen > 3
      Pic = "@B $" + REPLICATE("9",NLen-3)
ENDCASE
@ PRow, PCol+NBlanks SAY Num PICTURE "&Pic"
RETURN
*END:DFLOATI
```

Comments:

This Procedure builds a macro for the PICTURE clause
in an @ **X,Y SAY** statement. By inserting the appropriate
number of blanks, and using the computer PICTURE
clause, a floating dollar sign is simulated.

DISPLAYING DOLLARS AND CENTS
The problem:

You have to display a dollar amount on the screen. The number can be between $10.00 and $10,000,000.00. When you try to print the number, you find that you can print either: $$$$$$$$$10.00 or $ 10.00, if you leave enough room for the ten million dollar figure. What are you going to do?

The solution:

Write a Procedure to print a floating point number with a floating dollar sign and commas.

The calling code:

```
*   . . .
    SET COLOR TO &ColStand
    CLEAR
    X = 1234.12
    Y = 1234567.34
    Z = 12.63
    @ 10,0 SAY "123456789012345678901234567890"
    @ 11,5 SAY X PICTURE "$999,999,999.99"
    DO DFLOATF WITH 12, 5, 15, X
    DO DFLOATF WITH 13, 5, 15, Y
    DO DFLOATF WITH 14, 5, 15, Z
*   . . .
```

The Procedure:

```
PROCEDURE DFLOATF
*
*  Program...: DFLOATF
*  Author....: Phil Steele - President
*             Phillipps Computer Systems Inc.
*  Address...: 52 Hook Mountain Road,
*             Montville NJ 07045
*  Phone.....: (201) 575-8575
*  Date......: 01/02/89
*  Notice....: Copyright 1989  Philip Steele,
*             All Rights Reserved.
*  Notes.....: This procedure places a dollar sign
*             next to the high order digit of a
*             floating point number with no
*             no intervening spaces. Eg. $1,234.56
*  Parameters: PRow - The row to print the number on.
*             PCol - The col where the high order
*                    digit of the largest number
*                    would print.
*             FLen - The length of the picture
*                    clause.
*             Num  - The number to print with a
*                    leading dollar sign.
*
PARAMETERS PRow, PCol, FLen, Num
PRIVATE    PRow, PCol, FLen, Num, NLen, NBlanks
NLen    = LEN(LTRIM(STR(Num,19,2)))
NBlanks = FLen - NLen - 4
DO CASE
   CASE NLen > 9
      NBlanks = NBlanks + 1
      Pic = "@B $"+REPLICATE("9",NLen-9)+",999,999.99"
   CASE NLen > 6
      NBlanks = NBlanks + 2
      Pic = "@B $"+REPLICATE("9",NLen-6)+",999.99"
   CASE NLen > 3
      NBlanks = NBlanks + 3
      Pic = "@B $"+REPLICATE("9",NLen-3)+".99"
ENDCASE
@ PRow, PCol+NBlanks SAY Num PICTURE "&Pic"
RETURN
*END:DFLOATF
```

Comments:

This UDF builds a macro for the PICTURE clause in an @ **X,Y SAY** statement. By inserting the appropriate number of blanks, and using the computer PICTURE clause, a floating dollar sign is simulated.

6

Reports

Most of the preceding User-Defined Functions can be used for reports as well as for screen displays. However, there are unique problems associated with reports, and unique User-Defined Functions have been developed to manage them.

HORIZONTAL LINES ON A LASER PRINTER

The problem:

Most of my clients are using laser printers in their organizations. At various times, it is necessary to draw horizontal lines on a laser printer from within a dBASE IV application. The Hewlett-Packard command language is quite complex. What will I do?

The solution:

Write a User-Defined Function to simplify the printing of horizontal lines.

The calling code:

```
*    . . .
     SET COLOR TO &ColStand
     CLEAR
     SET DEVICE TO PRINT
               N     = 0
               Esc   = CHR(27)
               Start = Esc + "*p0x0Y"
     @ N,0 SAY "&Start"
     HorLine = HLine(1, 2, 6, 2)
     @ N,0 SAY "&HorLine"
     EJECT
     SET DEVICE TO SCREEN
*    . . .
```

The User-Defined Function:

```
FUNCTION HLINE
*
*  | Program...: HLINE
*  | Author....: Phil Steele - President
*  |             Phillipps Computer Systems Inc.
*  | Address...: 52 Hook Mountain Road,
*  |             Montville NJ 07045
*  | Phone.....: (201) 575-8575
*  | Date......: 01/02/89
*  | Notice....: Copyright 1989  Philip Steele,
*  |             All Rights Reserved.
*  | Notes.....: This function returns the HP laser jet
*  |             code needed to print a horizontal line
*  | Parameters: StartD - The starting position of the
*  |                      line down from the top of the
*  |                      page in inches.
*  |             StartL - The starting position of the
*  |                      line in from the left of the
*  |                      page in inches.
*  |             HLen   - The length of the horizontal
*  |                      line in inches.
*  |             LWidth - The width of the horizontal
*  |                      line in 1/300's of an inch.
*
PARAMETERS StartD, StartL, HLen, LWidth
PRIVATE    CompD,  CompL,  CLen, Esc
Esc      = CHR(27)
CompD    = 300 * StartD - 150
CompD    = IIF(CompD<0, 0, CompD)
CompL    = 300 * StartL - 75
CompL    = IIF(CompL<0, 0, CompL)
CLen     = 300 * HLen
HorLine = Esc + "*p" + STR(CompD,5,0) + ;
          "y" + STR(CompL,5,0) + "X" + ;
          Esc + "*c" + STR(LWidth,2,0) + ;
          "b" + STR(CLen, 5,0) + "a0P"
RETURN(HorLine)
*END:HLINE
```

Comments:

This UDF computes the starting position of the line, to be drawn at a scale of 300 to the inch, and subtracts the standard margins from the results. It returns the computed string, where it is printed by the calling routine. The DEVICE must be set to PRINT by the calling procedure.

VERTICAL LINES ON A LASER PRINTER

The problem:

> A client is using laser printers in her organization. At various times, you find it necessary to draw vertical lines using the laser printer from within a dBASE IV application. The Hewlett-Packard command language is quite complex. What will you do?

The solution:

> Write a User-Defined Function to simplify the printing of vertical lines.

The calling code:

```
*   . . .
    SET COLOR TO &ColStand
    CLEAR
    SET DEVICE TO PRINT
    N     = 0
    Esc   = CHR(27)
    Start = Esc +  "*p0x0Y"
    @ N,0 SAY "&Start"
    VerLine = VLine(1, 2, 6, 2)
    @ N,0 SAY "&VerLine"
    EJECT
    SET DEVICE TO SCREEN
*   . . .
```

The User-Defined Function:

```
FUNCTION VLINE
*┌─────────────────────────────────────────────────────┐
*│ Program...: VLINE                                     │
*│ Author....: Phil Steele - President                   │
*│             Phillipps Computer Systems Inc.           │
*│ Address...: 52 Hook Mountain Road,                    │
*│             Montville NJ 07045                        │
*│ Phone.....: (201) 575-8575                            │
*│ Date......: 01/02/89                                  │
*│ Notice....: Copyright 1989  Philip Steele,            │
*│             All Rights Reserved.                      │
*│ Notes.....: This function returns the HP laser jet    │
*│             code needed to print a vertical line.     │
*│ Parameters: StartD - The starting position of the     │
*│                      line down from the top of the    │
*│                      page in inches.                  │
*│             StartL - The starting position of the     │
*│                      line in from the left of the     │
*│                      page in inches.                  │
*│             VLen   - The length of the vertical       │
*│                      line in inches.                  │
*│             LWidth - The width of the vertical        │
*│                      line in 1/300's of an inch.      │
*└─────────────────────────────────────────────────────┘
PARAMETERS StartD, StartL, VLen, LWidth
PRIVATE    CompD,  CompL,  CLen, Esc
Esc     = CHR(27)
CompD   = 300 * StartD - 150
CompD   = IIF(CompD<0, 0, CompD)
CompL   = 300 * StartL - 75
CompL   = IIF(CompL<0, 0, CompL)
CLen    = 300 * VLen
VerLine = Esc + "*p" + STR(CompD,5,0) + ;
          "y" + STR(CompL,5,0) + "X" + ;
          Esc + "*c" + STR(LWidth,2,0) + ;
          "a" + STR(CLen, 5,0) + "b0P"
RETURN(VerLine)
*END:VLINE
```

Comments:

This UDF computes the starting position of the line, to be drawn at a scale of 300 to the inch, and subtracts the standard margins from the results. It returns the computed string, where it is printed by the calling routine. The DEVICE must be set to PRINT by the calling procedure.

BOXES ON A LASER PRINTER

The problem:

A client is using a laser printer in her organization. At various times, you find it necessary to create forms for her from within dBASE IV. Some of these forms contain boxes, and the Hewlett-Packard command language is quite complex. What will you do?

The solution:

Write a Procedure to simplify the printing of boxes.

The calling code:

```
*   . . .
    SET COLOR TO &ColStand
    CLEAR
    SET DEVICE TO PRINT
    N     = 0
    Esc   = CHR(27)
    Start = Esc + "*p0x0Y"
    @ N,0 SAY "&Start"
    DO HPBox WITH 1, 2, 5, 3, 2, N
    EJECT
    SET DEVICE TO SCREEN
*   . . .
```

The Procedure:

```
PROCEDURE HPBOX
*
* Program...: HPBOX
* Author....: Phil Steele - President
*             Phillipps Computer Systems Inc.
* Address...: 52 Hook Mountain Road,
*             Montville NJ 07045
* Phone.....: (201) 575-8575
* Date......: 01/02/89
* Notice....: Copyright 1989  Philip Steele,
*             All Rights Reserved.
* Notes.....: This procedure draws a box on a laser
*             printer.
* Parameters: StartD - The starting position of the
*                      box down from the top of the
*                      top of the page in inches.
*             StartL - The starting position of the
*                      box in from the left of the
*                      page in inches.
*             EndD   - The ending position of the
*                      box down from the top of the
*                      top of the page in inches.
*             EndR   - The ending position of the
*                      box in from the left of the
*                      page in inches.
*             LWidth - The width of the vertical
*                      line in 1/300's of an inch.
*             J      - The line current line number
*                      where printing is occurring.
*
PARAMETERS StartD, StartL, EndD, EndR, LWidth, J
PRIVATE    HStart, HLen, VStart, VLen, HStart2,;
           VStart2, Esc, T, L, B, R
Esc     = CHR(27)
HStart  = StartD
HLen    = EndD - StartD
VStart  = StartL
VLen    = EndR - StartL
HStart2 = EndD
VStart2 = EndR
T = HLine(HStart,  VStart,  VLen, LWidth)
R = VLine(HStart,  VStart,  HLen, LWidth)
B = HLine(HStart2, VStart,  VLen, LWidth)
L = VLine(HStart,  VStart2, HLen, LWidth)
@ J, 0 SAY "&T"
@ J, 0 SAY "&R"
@ J, 0 SAY "&B"
@ J, 0 SAY "&L"
RETURN
*END:HPBOX
```

Comments:

This UDF computes the starting positions and lengths of the lines needed to be drawn to make a box, and then calls the previously written User-Defined Functions to draw the box.

SHADING ON A LASER PRINTER

The problem:

A client is using a laser printer in his organization. At various times you find it necessary to create forms for him from within dBASE IV. Some of these forms contain large vertical and horizontal shaded areas. What will you do?

The solution:

Write a User-Defined Function to simplify the printing of shaded areas.

The calling code:

```
*    . . .
     SET COLOR TO &ColStand
     CLEAR
     SET DEVICE TO PRINT
     N      = 0
     Esc    = CHR(27)
     Start  = Esc + "*p0x0Y"
 @ N,0 SAY "&Start"
*  *  * Horizontal shaded area *  *  *
     Shade = Shady(1, 2, 6, .5, 30)
     @ N,0 SAY "&Shade"
*  *  * Vertical shaded area *  *  *
     Shade = Shady(1, 2, .5, 6, 30)
     @ N,0 SAY "&Shade"
     EJECT
     SET DEVICE TO SCREEN
*    . . .
```

The User-Defined Function:

```
FUNCTION SHADY
*
*┌─────────────────────────────────────────────────────────────┐
*│ Program...: SHADY                                             │
*│ Author....: Phil Steele - President                          │
*│            Phillipps Computer Systems Inc.                   │
*│ Address...: 52 Hook Mountain Road,                           │
*│            Montville NJ 07045                                │
*│ Phone.....: (201) 575-8575                                   │
*│ Date......: 01/02/89                                         │
*│ Notice....: Copyright 1989  Philip Steele,                  │
*│            All Rights Reserved.                             │
*│ Notes.....: This function returns the HP laser jet           │
*│            code needed to print a shaded line of            │
*│            any length or width.                             │
*│ Parameters: StartD - The starting position of the            │
*│                      gray line down from the top            │
*│                      of the page in inches.                 │
*│            StartL - The starting position of the            │
*│                      gray line in from the left of          │
*│                      the page in inches.                    │
*│            HLen   - The length of the shaded line           │
*│                      in inches.                             │
*│            LWidth - The width of the shaded line            │
*│                      in inches.                             │
*└─────────────────────────────────────────────────────────────┘
*
PARAMETERS StartD, StartL, HLen, LWidth, Pct
PRIVATE      CompD,  CompL,  CLen, Esc
Esc       = CHR(27)
CompD     = 300 * StartD - 150
CompD     = IIF(CompD<0, 0, CompD)
CompL     = 300 * StartL - 75
CompL     = IIF(CompL<0, 0, CompL)
CLen      = 300 * HLen
LWidth    = 300 * LWidth
Shades    = Esc + "*p" + STR(CompD,5,0)  + "y" + ;
            STR(CompL,5,0) + "X" + ;
            Esc + "*c" + STR(LWidth,6,0) + "b" + ;
            STR(CLen, 5,0) + "a" + STR(Pct,2,0) + "g2P"
RETURN(Shades)
*END:SHADE
```

Comments:

This UDF computes the starting position of the line, to be drawn at a scale of 300 to the inch, and subtracts the standard margins from the results. It returns the computed string where it is printed by the calling procedure. The DEVICE must be set to PRINT by the calling procedure. By using a small number for the length, and a large number for the width, a vertical shaded area will be created (case two in the calling procedure).

GRAPHS

The problem:

A client is using laser printers in her organization. At various times, you find it necessary to create graphs with different fill patterns from within dBASE IV. Some of these graphs are vertical, and some are horizontal. What will you do?

The solution:

Write a User-Defined Function to simplify the printing of graphs.

The calling code:

```
*    . . .
     SET COLOR TO &ColStand
     CLEAR
     SET DEVICE TO PRINT
         N    = 0
         Esc  = CHR(27)
         Start = Esc + "*p0x0Y"
   @ N,0 SAY "&Start"
* * * Horizontal bar graph * * *
   Patt = Pattern(1, 2, 6, .5, 4)
   @ N,0 SAY "&Patt"
* * * Vertical bar graph * * *
   Patt = Pattern(1, 2, .5, 6, 5)
   @ N,0 SAY "&Patt"
   EJECT
   SET DEVICE TO SCREEN
*    . . .
```

The User-Defined Function:

```
FUNCTION PATTERN
*┌────────────────────────────────────────────────────────────┐
* │  Program...: PATTERN                                        │
* │  Author....: Phil Steele - President                        │
* │              Phillipps Computer Systems Inc.                │
* │  Address...: 52 Hook Mountain Road,                         │
* │              Montville NJ 07045                             │
* │  Phone.....: (201) 575-8575                                 │
* │  Date......: 01/02/89                                       │
* │  Notice....: Copyright 1989  Philip Steele,                 │
* │              All Rights Reserved.                           │
* │  Notes.....: This function returns the HP laser jet         │
* │              code needed to print one of the six           │
* │              HP defined patterns.                           │
* │  Parameters: StartD - The starting position of the          │
* │                       pattern down from the top of          │
* │                       the page in inches.                   │
* │              StartL - The starting position of the          │
* │                       pattern in from the left of           │
* │                       the page in inches.                   │
* │              HLen   - The length of the pattern in          │
* │                       inches.                               │
* │              LWidth - The width of the pattern in           │
* │                       inches.                               │
*└────────────────────────────────────────────────────────────┘
*
PARAMETERS StartD, StartL, HLen, LWidth, Pat
PRIVATE      CompD,  CompL,  CLen, Esc
Esc      = CHR(27)
CompD    = 300 * StartD - 150
CompD    = IIF(CompD<0, 0, CompD)
CompL    = 300 * StartL - 75
CompL    = IIF(CompL<0, 0, CompL)
CLen     = 300 * HLen
LWidth   = 300 * LWidth
Patt     = Esc + "*p" + STR(CompD,5,0)  + "y" + ;
               STR(CompL,5,0) + "X" + ;
               Esc + "*c" + STR(LWidth,6,0) + "b" + ;
               STR(CLen, 5,0) + "a" + STR(Pat,2,0) + "g3P"
RETURN(Patt)
*END:PATTERN
```

Comments:

This UDF computes the starting position of the bar, to be drawn at a scale of 300 to the inch, and subtracts the standard margins from the results. It returns the computed string where it is printed by the calling procedure. The DEVICE must be set to PRINT by the calling procedure. By using a small number for the length, and a large number for the width, a vertical bar will be created (case two in the calling procedure).

Note: You can create additional patterns by combining the six HP defined patterns. Look at the upper left corner of the example.

LEFT-JUSTIFYING

The problem:

In many reports you find you have to left-justify a string and still retain the length of string. PICTURE @B does not work with a string. What will you do?

The solution:

Write the following User-Defined Function to perform this needed function.

The calling code:

```
*     . . .
      SET COLOR TO &ColStand
      CLEAR
      FName  = "   PHIL"
      LName  = "   STEELE"
      Name   = LJust(FName) + LJust(LName)
      ? Name
      ? Len(Name)
*     Len(Name) SHOULD = 18
*     . . .
```

The User-Defined Function:

```
FUNCTION LJUST
*
*   Program...: LJUST
*   Author....: Phil Steele - President
*             Phillipps Computer Systems Inc.
*   Address...: 52 Hook Mountain Road,
*             Montville NJ 07045
*   Phone.....: (201) 575-8575
*   Date......: 01/02/89
*   Notice....: Copyright 1989  Philip Steele,
*             All Rights Reserved.
*   Notes.....: This function left justifies a string.
*   Parameters: InStr - The string to left justify.
*
PARAMETERS InStr
PRIVATE N, OutStr
N      = LEN(InStr)
OutStr = LTRIM(InStr)
OutStr = OutStr + REPLICATE(" ", N-LEN(OutStr))
RETURN(OutStr)
*END:LJUST
```

Comments:

This UDF left-justifies a field by left-trimming the field, and appending blanks to the right end of the field. The number of blanks is equal to the length of the original field minus the length of the trimmed blanks.

SOMETHING LIKE *SUBSTR*

The problem:

> While working with a report, you had to remove the employee's middle name from the name field in the database before printing it.

The solution:

> Write a User-Defined Function that works like SUBSTR—except that, instead of returning the selected portion of the string, it returns the remainder of the string.

The calling code:

```
*   . . .
    SET COLOR TO &ColStand
    CLEAR
    Str     = "THIS IS A LONG STRING"
    NewStr  = REMOVE(Str,11,5)
  ? NewStr
*   . . .
```

The User-Defined Function:

```
FUNCTION REMOVE
*
*  Program...: REMOVE
*  Author....: Phil Steele - President
*              Phillipps Computer Systems Inc.
*  Address...: 52 Hook Mountain Road,
*              Montville NJ 07045
*  Phone.....: (201) 575-8575
*  Date......: 01/02/89
*  Notice....: Copyright 1989  Philip Steele,
*              All Rights Reserved.
*  Notes.....: This function removes a group of
*              characters from a string.
*  Parameters: Str   - The string to operate on.
*              Start - The starting position of the
*                      area to be removed.
*              RLen  - The length of the area to
*                      remove.
*
PARAMETERS Str, Start, RLen
PRIVATE    Str, Start, RLen, NewStr
NewStr = SUBSTR(Str,1,Start-1) + SUBSTR(Str,Start+RLen)
RETURN (NewStr)
*END:REMOVE
```

Comments:

This UDF works like SUBSTR in reverse: it returns the string without the selected portion.

UPPER- AND LOWERCASING
The problem:

> While working with the previous report, not only did you have to remove the employee's middle name, but you also had to change the way it was printed. In the database, it was in all uppercase; in the report, the initial character must be in uppercase, and the remaining characters in lowercase.

The solution:

> Write a User-Defined Function to perform this operation.

The calling code:

```
*   . . .
    SET COLOR TO &ColStand
    CLEAR
    A  =  "phil"
    B  =  "PHIL"
    X  =  PROPER(A)
    ? X
    X  =  PROPER(B)
    ? X
*   . . .
```

The User-Defined Function:

```
FUNCTION PROPER
*
* | Program...: PROPER
* | Author....: Phil Steele - President
* |            Phillipps Computer Systems Inc.
* | Address...: 52 Hook Mountain Road,
* |            Montville NJ 07045
* | Phone.....: (201) 575-8575
* | Date......: 01/02/89
* | Notice....: Copyright 1989  Philip Steele,
* |            All Rights Reserved.
* | Notes.....: This function converts a string to
* |            lower case and then converts the first
* |            character of the string to upper case.
* | Parameters: X - The words to convert into "proper"
* |                format.
*
PARAMETERS X
X = UPPER(SUBSTR(X,1,1)) + LOWER(SUBSTR(X,2))
RETURN(X)
*END:PROPER
```

Comments:

This UDF changes the first character of the string to uppercase using the dBASE IV built-in functions UPPER and SUBSTR, and the remainder of the string to lowercase using the dBASE IV built-in functions LOWER and SUBSTR.

POSTAL STATE ABBREVIATIONS

The problem:

> While working with a national company, letters must
> be sent to various states. The clerical staff mixes up the
> state abbreviation codes. You are required to provide the
> code that will permit a clerk to determine the state from
> the abbreviation, or vice versa.

The solution:

> Write a User-Defined Function to perform this operation.

The calling code:

```
*   . . .
    SET COLOR TO &ColStand
    CLEAR
    X  =   "MO"
    Y  =   "Montana"
    Z  =   "XX"
    STORE " " TO State, Abv
    DO StateAbv WITH X, "N", State
    @ 11,20 SAY X + " is the abbreviation for " + State
    DO StateAbv WITH Y, "A", Abv
    @ 13,20 SAY Abv + " is the abbreviation for " + Y
    DO StateAbv WITH Z, "N", State
    @ 15,20 SAY Z +  "is the abbreviation for " + State
*   . . .
```

The Procedure:

```
PROCEDURE STATEABV
*┌──────────────────────────────────────────────────────────┐
*│ Program...: STATEABV                                      │
*│ Author....: Phil Steele - President                      │
*│            Phillipps Computer Systems Inc.               │
*│ Address...: 52 Hook Mountain Road,                       │
*│            Montville NJ 07045                            │
*│ Phone.....: (201) 575-8575                               │
*│ Date......: 01/02/89                                     │
*│ Notice....: Copyright 1989  Philip Steele,               │
*│            All Rights Reserved.                          │
*│ Notes.....: This procedure returns the two letter        │
*│            abbreviation for a state name, or the         │
*│            state name given a two letter state           │
*│            abbreviation.                                 │
*│ Parameters: State - Either the two letter state          │
*│                    abbreviation or the state name.       │
*│            NorA  - "N" = return the state name.          │
*│                  - "A" = return the abbreviation.        │
*│            SNA   - Returned value.                       │
*└──────────────────────────────────────────────────────────┘
*
PARAMETERS State, NorA, SNA
PRIVATE Ans
PUBLIC ARRAY StateA[51], StateN[51]
StateA[ 1] = "AL"
StateA[ 2] = "AK"
StateA[ 3] = "AZ"
StateA[ 4] = "AR"
StateA[ 5] = "CA"
StateA[ 6] = "CO"
StateA[ 7] = "CT"
StateA[ 8] = "DE"
StateA[ 9] = "DC"
StateA[10] = "FL"
StateA[11] = "GA"
StateA[12] = "HI"
StateA[13] = "ID"
StateA[14] = "IL"
StateA[15] = "IN"
StateA[16] = "IA"
StateA[17] = "KS"
StateA[18] = "KY"
StateA[19] = "LA"
StateA[20] = "ME"
StateA[21] = "MD"
StateA[22] = "MA"
StateA[23] = "MI"
StateA[24] = "MN"
StateA[25] = "MS"
StateA[26] = "MO"
StateA[27] = "MT"
StateA[28] = "NE"
StateA[29] = "NV"
```

```
StateA[30] = "NH"
StateA[31] = "NJ"
StateA[32] = "NM"
StateA[33] = "NY"
StateA[34] = "NC"
StateA[35] = "ND"
StateA[36] = "OH"
StateA[37] = "OK"
StateA[38] = "OR"
StateA[39] = "PA"
StateA[40] = "RI"
StateA[41] = "SC"
StateA[42] = "SD"
StateA[43] = "TN"
StateA[44] = "TX"
StateA[45] = "UT"
StateA[46] = "VT"
StateA[47] = "VA"
StateA[48] = "WA"
StateA[49] = "WV"
StateA[50] = "WI"
StateA[51] = "WY"
StateN[ 1] = "Alabama"
StateN[ 2] = "Alaska"
StateN[ 3] = "Arizona"
StateN[ 4] = "Arkansas"
StateN[ 5] = "California"
StateN[ 6] = "Colorado"
StateN[ 7] = "Connecticut"
StateN[ 8] = "Delaware"
StateN[ 9] = "Dist of Columbia"
StateN[10] = "Florida"
StateN[11] = "Georgia"
StateN[12] = "Hawaii"
StateN[13] = "Idaho"
StateN[14] = "Illinois"
StateN[15] = "Indiana"
StateN[16] = "Iowa"
StateN[17] = "Kansas"
StateN[18] = "Kentucky"
StateN[19] = "Louisiana"
StateN[20] = "Maine"
StateN[21] = "Maryland"
StateN[22] = "Massachusetts"
StateN[23] = "Michigan"
StateN[24] = "Minnesota"
StateN[25] = "Mississippi"
StateN[26] = "Missouri"
StateN[27] = "Montana"
StateN[28] = "Nebraska"
StateN[29] = "Nevada"
StateN[30] = "New Hampshire"
StateN[31] = "New Jersey"
StateN[32] = "New Mexico"
StateN[33] = "New York"
StateN[34] = "North Carolina"
```

```
StateN[35] = "North Dakota"
StateN[36] = "Ohio"
StateN[37] = "Oklahoma"
StateN[38] = "Oregon"
StateN[39] = "Pennsylvania"
StateN[40] = "Rhode Island"
StateN[41] = "South Carolina"
StateN[42] = "South Dakota"
StateN[43] = "Tennessee"
StateN[44] = "Texas"
StateN[45] = "Utah"
StateN[46] = "Vermont"
StateN[47] = "Virginia"
StateN[48] = "Washington"
StateN[49] = "West Virginia"
StateN[50] = "Wisconsin"
StateN[51] = "Wyoming"
Ans = 0
IF NorA = "N"
   DO AScan WITH "StateA", "&State", 1, 51, Ans
   SNA = IIF(Ans<>0, StateN[Ans], "Does NOT exist!")
ELSE
   DO AScan WITH "StateN", "&State", 1, 51, Ans
   SNA = IIF(Ans<>0, StateA[Ans], "Does NOT exist!")
ENDIF
RETURN
*END:STATEABV
```

Comments:

This UDF uses two arrays: one for the abbreviation, and another for the state. The Procedure ASCAN, which we developed in the ARRAY section, is used to find the position of the input in the array. The output is at the same location in the other array. The array element located at this location is returned to the calling program.

DISREGARDING CASE FOR COMPARISON

The problem:

> We have to compare two databases: one with all
> uppercase variables, and the other containing variables
> in both upper- and lowercase. We need to determine if
> the data is the same, regardless of case.

The solution:

> Write a User-Defined Function to perform this operation.

The calling code:

```
*   . . .
    SET COLOR TO &ColStand
    CLEAR
    A  =   "Phil"
    B  =   "PHIL"
    C  =   "PHILL"
    D  =   "Bill"
    X  =   COMPARE(A,B)
    ? X
    X  =   COMPARE(A,C)
    ? X
    X  =   COMPARE(A,D)
    ? X
*   . . .
```

The User-Defined Function:

```
FUNCTION COMPARE
*
*  ┌─────────────────────────────────────────────────────┐
*  │ Program...: COMPARE                                  │
*  │ Author....: Phil Steele - President                 │
*  │            Phillipps Computer Systems Inc.          │
*  │ Address...: 52 Hook Mountain Road,                  │
*  │            Montville NJ 07045                        │
*  │ Phone.....: (201) 575-8575                           │
*  │ Date......: 01/02/89                                 │
*  │ Notice....: Copyright 1989  Philip Steele,          │
*  │            All Rights Reserved.                     │
*  │ Notes.....: This function draws a horizontal line   │
*  │            on a laser printer.                      │
*  │ Parameters: X - The first variable to compare.      │
*  │            Y - The second variable to compare.     │
*  └─────────────────────────────────────────────────────┘
*
PARAMETERS X, Y
PRIVATE     X, Y, Ret
SET EXACT ON
Ret = IIF(UPPER(X)=UPPER(Y), .T., .F.)
SET EXACT OFF
RETURN(Ret)
*END:COMPARE
```

Comments:

This UDF changes both variables to uppercase, performs the compare, and returns the result as either a TRUE (they compare) or FALSE (they do not compare).

7

Conversions

I wrote a large system for an international organization that required all of the commonly used measurements to be printed using metric system values internationally and American values stateside.

To illustrate these conversions, I have chosen a UDF that converts kilometers-to-miles and miles-to-kilometers. To convert other units of measure, you only have to change the conversion numbers. For example, if you want to convert meters-to-feet, you must change KMeterMil from 0.621... to 3.280... and MilesKMet from 1.609... to 0.304... and, for readability, change the names of the variables (KMeterMil to MeterFoot, and MilesKMet to FootMeter). This method will work, no matter what the conversion, as long as the relationship is mathematically linear.

KILOMETERS AND MILES

The problem:

The first conversion needed was kilometers-to-miles and miles-to-kilometers.

The solution:

Develop User-Defined Functions that could compute the appropriate values, depending upon where the system is run.

The calling code:

```
*  . . .
   SET COLOR TO &ColStand
   SET DECIMALS TO 5
   CLEAR
   X  =  1
   NewValue  =   KmMile(X,"A")
   ? X
   ? NewValue
*   . . .
```

The User-Defined Function:

```
FUNCTION KMMILE
*
* | Program...: KMMILE
* | Author....: Phil Steele - President
* |              Phillipps Computer Systems Inc.
* | Address...: 52 Hook Mountain Road,
* |              Montville NJ 07045
* | Phone.....: (201) 575-8575
* | Date......: 01/02/89
* | Notice....: Copyright 1989  Philip Steele,
* |              All Rights Reserved.
* | Notes.....: This function converts kilometers to
* |              miles and miles to kilometers.
* | Parameters: X  - The variable to be converted from
* |                  metric or American to the other.
* |              MA - "M" = convert to metric.
* |                   "A" = convert to American.
*
PARAMETERS X, MA
PRIVATE    FactorM, FactorA, Factor
KMeterMil = 0.6213699495
MilesKMet = 1.609347219
FactorM   = KMeterMil
FactorA   = MilesKMet
Factor    = IIF(UPPER(MA)="A", FactorM, FactorA)
RETURN(X * Factor)
*END:KMMILE
```

Comments:

This User-Defined Function checks which way the conversion is to take place (metric-to-American, or American-to-metric), places the correct value into the "Factor" variable, and proceeds with the conversion.

Note:

A value of "A" converts from metric to American, and a value of "M" converts from American to metric.

I use the term *American* not *English* because there is a difference in some measurements between American and English, such as with a gallon.

CENTIGRADE AND FAHRENHEIT

The problem:

The next conversion needed was centigrade-to-Fahrenheit and Fahrenheit-to-centigrade.

The solution:

Develop User-Defined Functions that will compute the appropriate values, depending upon where the system is run.

The calling code:

```
*  . . .
SET COLOR TO &ColStand
CLEAR
X  =  40
NewValue  =   CentF(X,"M")
? "40 C"
? STR(NewValue,3,0)  +  " F"
? " "
X  =  212
NewValue  =   CentF(X,"A")
? "212 F"
? STR(NewValue,3,0)  +  "  C"
*  . . .
```

The User-Defined Function:

```
FUNCTION CENTF
*┌──────────────────────────────────────────────────────────┐
*│ Program...: CENTF                                          │
*│ Author....: Phil Steele - President                        │
*│            Phillipps Computer Systems Inc.                 │
*│ Address...: 52 Hook Mountain Road,                         │
*│            Montville NJ 07045                              │
*│ Phone.....: (201) 575-8575                                 │
*│ Date......: 01/02/89                                       │
*│ Notice....: Copyright 1989  Philip Steele,                 │
*│            All Rights Reserved.                            │
*│ Notes.....: This function converts centigrade to           │
*│            Fahrenheit and Fahrenheit to                    │
*│            centigrade.                                     │
*│ Parameters: X  - The variable to be converted from         │
*│                 metric or American to the other.          │
*│            MA - "M" = convert to metric.                   │
*│                 "A" = convert to American.                │
*└──────────────────────────────────────────────────────────┘
PARAMETERS X, MA
PRIVATE    FactorM, FactorA, Answer
Centigrade = (X - 32) * 5 / 9
Fahrenheit = (X * 9 /5) + 32
FactorM    = Centigrade
FactorA    = Fahrenheit
Answer     = IIF(UPPER(MA)="A", FactorM, FactorA)
RETURN(Answer)
*END:CENTF
```

Comments:

This User-Defined Function checks which way the conversion is to take place (metric-to-American, or American-to metric), places the correct value into the "Factor" variable, and proceeds with the conversion.

8

Miscellaneous

This section contains User-Defined Functions that can't be classified in any other area.

CREATING A FILE

The problem:

When we wrote the ADIR function in the array portion of this book, we had to create a database from within a procedure. A new "DBF" file is needed to hold some temporary data that is dependent on the user. You do not want to leave this file on the disk when you are finished; therefore, it is not available when you need it. What are you going to do?

The solution:

Write a Procedure to create a file from inside of a procedure.

The calling code:

```
*    . . .
     SET COLOR TO &ColStand
     CLEAR
     OldN       = "SAMPLES½EMPLOYEE"
     NewName = "ADIR"
     PUBLIC ARRAY FName[2]
     PUBLIC ARRAY FType[2]
     PUBLIC ARRAY FLen [2]
     PUBLIC ARRAY FDec [2]
     FName [1]   = "FName"
     FName [2]   = "Ext"
     FType [1]   = "C"
     FType [2]   = "C"
     FLen [1]    = 9
     FLen [2]    = 3
     FDec [1]    = 0
     FDec [2]    = 0
     DO MakeF WITH OldN, NewName, 2
     DISPLAY STRUCTURE
*    . . .
```

The Procedure:

```
PROCEDURE MAKEF
*
*   Program...: MAKEF
*   Author....: Phil Steele - President
*             Phillipps Computer Systems Inc.
*   Address...: 52 Hook Mountain Road,
*             Montville NJ 07045
*   Phone.....: (201) 575-8575
*   Date......: 01/02/89
*   Notice....: Copyright 1989   Philip Steele,
*             All Rights Reserved.
*   Notes.....: This function creates a new DBF file
*             from 4 arrays
*   Parameters: OldN    - The name of an existing DBF
*                         file.
*               NewN    - The name of the DBF file to
*                         create.
*               FNumber - The number of fields in the
*                         new file.
*               FName   - A PUBLIC array containing
*                         field names for the new file.
*               FType   - A PUBLIC array containing
*                         field types.
*               FLen    - A PUBLIC array containing
*                         field lengths.
*               FDec    - A PUBLIC array containing
*                         the number of decimal points.
*
PARAMETERS OldN, NewN, FNumber
PRIVATE    OldN, NewN, FNumber, N
USE &OldN
COPY TO TEMP STRUCTURE EXTENDED
USE TEMP
ZAP
N = 1
DO WHILE N <= FNumber
   APPEND BLANK
   REPLACE Field_Name WITH FName[N]
   REPLACE Field_Type WITH FType[N]
   REPLACE Field_Len  WITH FLen[N]
   REPLACE Field_Dec  WITH FDec[N]
   N = N + 1
ENDDO
CREATE &NewN FROM TEMP
RUN DEL TEMP.DBF >NUL
RETURN
*END:MAKEF
```

Comments:

This Procedure uses an existing file to create the new
one. In this example, it uses the file "Employee" located
in the sample sub-directory, which is created when you
install dBASE IV. It also uses arrays containing the field
names, lengths and types. It copies the existing file to
a "STRUCTURE EXTENDED" file. A structure extended
file can be used to create a new file, or used as a data
dictionary. This file is "ZAPPED" and filled with the
values from the arrays. A normal DBF file is then created
from the structure extended file. The structure extended
file is deleted before returning to the calling procedure.

SWAP VARIABLES

The problem:

> While writing a sort function, you need to interchange two variables.

The solution:

> Write a User-Defined Function to swap two variables.

The calling code:

```
*    . . .
SET COLOR TO &ColStand
CLEAR
N  =  5
Z  =  4
? N, Z
A  =  SWAP(N, Z)
? N, Z
*    . . .
```

The User-Defined Function:

```
FUNCTION SWAP
*
*  Program...: SWAP
*  Author....: Phil Steele - President
*             Phillipps Computer Systems Inc.
*  Address...: 52 Hook Mountain Road,
*             Montville NJ 07045
*  Phone.....: (201) 575-8575
*  Date......: 01/02/89
*  Notice....: Copyright 1989  Philip Steele,
*             All Rights Reserved.
*  Notes.....: This function swaps the values of two
*             variables.
*  Parameters: A - A variable to be swapped.
*             B - Another variable to be swapped.
*
PARAMETERS A, B
PRIVATE    C
C = A
A = B
B = C
RETURN(.T.)
*END:SWAP
```

Comments:

This UDF is straightforward and uses an intermediate
variable to temporarily hold the contents of one of the
swapped variables.

ERROR DISPLAY: METHOD ONE

The problem:

In every system I have ever written, there is a need to tell the user when an error condition has occurred. This can be in data entry, in computation, or when various expected conditions do not occur. All error messages should appear on the screen in the same place, and in the same format, so that the user knows where to look if an error is suspected. They also should be in one place in your code so that you can easily change them.

Because this is such an important feature of all systems, I am including three different methods of displaying errors.

The solution:

Write a Procedure that displays error messages in a consistent manner.

The calling code:

```
*    . . .
     SET COLOR TO &ColStand
     CLEAR
     Test = .F.
     IF .NOT. Test
        DO ERR WITH 1, "&ColStand""
*    . . .
     ENDIF
*    . . .
```

The Procedure:

```
PROCEDURE ERR
*
*  Program...: ERR
*  Author....: Phil Steele - President
*             Phillipps Computer Systems Inc.
*  Address...: 52 Hook Mountain Road,
*             Montville NJ 07045
*  Phone.....: (201) 575-8575
*  Date......: 01/02/89
*  Notice....: Copyright 1989  Philip Steele,
*             All Rights Reserved.
*  Notes.....: This function save the screen and
*             displays a centered error message in
*             bright white on red at the bottom of
*             the screen for 5 seconds and then
*             restores the screen.
*  Parameters: N        - The number of the error
*                         to display.
*             OldColor - The original color of the
*                        screen display.
*
PARAMETERS N, OldColor
PRIVATE    Key
SET COLOR TO W+/R
@ 24,0
DO CASE
   CASE N = 1
      @ 24,0 SAY MessCent("Error Message one")
   CASE N = 2
      @ 24,0 SAY MessCent("Error Message two")
   CASE N = 3
      @ 24,0 SAY MessCent("Error Message three")
   CASE N = 4
      @ 24,0 SAY MessCent("Error Message four")
   CASE N = 5
      @ 24,0 SAY MessCent("Error Message five")
ENDCASE
Key = INKEY(5)
SET COLOR TO &ColStand
RETURN
*END:ERR
```

Comments:

This Procedure sets the colors to bright white on red (a very good choice for error messages), clears the last line of the screen, and finds the error to display using a CASE statement. It displays the error and waits for five seconds before restoring the screen colors and returning to the calling procedure.

Note: This Procedure uses the MessCent UDF.

ERROR DISPLAY: METHOD TWO

The problem:

> You need to display error messages from various parts of your system.

The solution:

> Write a User-Defined Function that displays error messages in a consistent manner.

The calling code:

```
*   . . .
    SET COLOR TO &ColStand
    CLEAR
    Test  =  .F.
    IF .NOT. Test
        SET COLOR TO &ColError
        DEFINE WINDOW ERR1 FROM 21,0 TO;
        23,79 DOUBLE COLOR W + = */R
     A  =  ERR1(1)
        SET COLOR TO &ColStand
    ENDIF
*   . . .
```

The User-Defined Function:

```
FUNCTION ERR1
*
* ┌─────────────────────────────────────────────────────────┐
* │ Program...: ERR1                                        │
* │ Author....: Phil Steele - President                     │
* │            Phillipps Computer Systems Inc.             │
* │ Address...: 52 Hook Mountain Road,                      │
* │            Montville NJ 07045                          │
* │ Phone.....: (201) 575-8575                              │
* │ Date......: 01/02/89                                    │
* │ Notice....: Copyright 1989  Philip Steele,             │
* │            All Rights Reserved.                        │
* │ Notes.....: This function saves the  screen  and       │
* │            displays a centered error  message in       │
* │            bright white on red at the bottom of        │
* │            the screen for 5 seconds and then           │
* │            restores the screen.                        │
* │ Parameters: N - The number of the error to display.    │
* └─────────────────────────────────────────────────────────┘
PARAMETERS N
ACTIVATE WINDOW ERR1
DO CASE
   CASE N = 1
      @ 0,0 SAY MessCent("Error Message one")
   CASE N = 2
      @ 0,0 SAY MessCent("Error Message two")
   CASE N = 3
      @ 0,0 SAY MessCent("Error Message three")
   CASE N = 4
      @ 0,0 SAY MessCent("Error Message four")
   CASE N = 5
      @ 0,0 SAY MessCent("Error Message five")
   OTHERWISE
      @ 0,0 SAY MessCent("An Error Has Occurred")
ENDCASE
Key = INKEY(5)
DEACTIVATE WINDOW ERR1
RELEASE     WINDOW ERR1
RETURN(.T.)
*END:ERR1
```

Comments:

This UDF relies upon the calling program to define a
window and draw a double line box into which the error
message is placed. If you write this Function as a
Procedure, you can define the window in the called
procedure rather than the calling procedure.

ERROR DISPLAY: METHOD THREE

The problem:

> You need to display dynamic error messages from various parts of your system.

The solution:

> Write a Procedure to display dynamic error messages.

The calling code:

```
*    . . .
   SET COLOR TO &ColStand
   CLEAR
   DO EXPERR WITH 1, "S"
*    . . .
```

The Procedure:

```
PROCEDURE EXPERR
*
*   Program...: EXPERR
*   Author....: Phil Steele - President
*               Phillipps Computer Systems Inc.
*   Address...: 52 Hook Mountain Road,
*               Montville NJ 07045
*   Phone.....: (201) 575-8575
*   Date......: 01/02/89
*   Notice....: Copyright 1989  Philip Steele,
*               All Rights Reserved.
*   Notes.....: This function produces an "exploding"
*               box at the bottom of the screen
*               containing an error message.
*   Parameters: NMess - The error message number.
*               DS    - Double or Single line box.
*
PARAMETERS NMess, DS
Private    NMess, DS, Kind, Mes
SET COLOR TO &ColError
Kind = IIF(DS="D", "Double", " ")
N = 39
DO WHILE N > 0
   @ 22,N CLEAR TO 24,79-N
   @ 22,N       TO 24,79-N &Kind
   N = N - 4
ENDDO
DO CASE
   CASE NMess = 1
      Mes = "Error Message one"
   CASE NMess = 2
      Mes = "Error Message two"
```

```
      CASE NMess = 3
         Mes = "Error Message three"
      CASE NMess = 4
         Mes = "Error Message four"
      CASE NMess = 5
         Mes = "Error Message five"
      OTHERWISE
         Mes = "An Error Has Occurred"
ENDCASE
@ 23, (80-LEN(Mes))/2 SAY Mes
Key = INKEY(5)
SET COLOR TO &ColStand
RETURN
*END:EXPERR
```

Comments:

> This UDF draws an "exploding" double- or single-line
> box at the bottom of the screen in bright white on red.
> It places the appropriate error message in this box. After
> five seconds, it sets the screen colors back to the stan-
> dard colors and returns to the calling procedure.

COUNTING STRING OCCURRENCES

The problem:

> You need to determine the number of occurrences of various special codes in a large string.

The solution:

> Develop a User-Defined Function that returns the number of times string one appears in string two.

The calling code:

```
*    . . .
SET COLOR TO &ColStand
CLEAR
X  =  "IS"
Y  =  "THIS IS A TEST OF HOWMANY"
Z  =  HowMany(X,Y)
? Z       && 2
*    . . .
```

The User-Defined Function:

```
FUNCTION HOWMANY
*
*   Program...: HOWMANY
*   Author....: Phil Steele - President
*               Phillipps Computer Systems Inc.
*   Address...: 52 Hook Mountain Road,
*               Montville NJ 07045
*   Phone.....: (201) 575-8575
*   Date......: 01/02/89
*   Notice....: Copyright 1989  Philip Steele,
*               All Rights Reserved.
*   Notes.....: This function returns the number of
*               times string one is found in string
*               two.
*   Parameters: Str1 - The string to look for.
*               Str2 - The string to look at to find
*                      Str1.
*
PARAMETERS Str1, Str2
Cnt = 0
DO WHILE AT(Str1, Str2) <> 0
   Cnt = Cnt + 1
   Str2 = SUBSTR(Str2, AT(Str1, Str2)+1)
ENDDO
RETURN(Cnt)
*END:HOWMANY
```

Comments:

This UDF uses a DO WHILE loop to count the number of times string one occurs in string two.

REMOVING BLANKS

The problem:

At times I found it necessary to remove both leading and trailing blanks from a string.

The solution:

Develop a User-Defined Function that removes leading and trailing blanks.

The calling code:

```
*   . . .
    SET COLOR TO &ColStand
    CLEAR
    X = "   Phil          "
    Y = "   Denise        "
    Z = "   Steele        "
    @ 12,30 SAY ALLTRIM(X)   +   " & " = ALLTRIM(Y)
               +  " ";  +  ALLTRIM(Z)

*   . . .
```

The User-Defined Function:

```
FUNCTION ALLTRIM
*
* Program...: ALLTRIM
* Author....: Phil Steele - President
*             Phillipps Computer Systems Inc.
* Address...: 52 Hook Mountain Road,
*             Montville NJ 07045
* Phone.....: (201) 575-8575
* Date......: 01/02/89
* Notice....: Copyright 1989  Philip Steele,
*             All Rights Reserved.
* Notes.....: This function returns the sting with
*             leading and trailing blanks removed.
* Parameters: String - The string to trim.
*
PARAMETER String
RETURN LTRIM(TRIM(String))
*END:ALLTRIM
```

Comments:

This UDF calls two dBASE IV functions, TRIM and LTRIM, to remove trailing and leading blanks.

SCREENING VALUES

The problem:

At times I found it necessary to determine if a field contains any value other than a null or blank during data entry.

The solution:

Develop a User-Defined Function that checks any type of field, and determines if it contains any value other than a blank or a null.

The calling code:

```
*   . . .
    SET COLOR TO &ColStand
    CLEAR
    X = 1
    ? "X = 1"
    ? EMPTY(X)
    X = FLOAT(0.0)
    ? "X = 0.0"
    ? EMPTY(X)
    Y = "    "
    ? "Y = '  '"
    ? EMPTY(Y)
    Z = { /  / }
    ? "Z = /  /  "
    ? EMPTY(Z)
    Z = {12/12/91}
    ? "Z = 12/12/91"
    ? EMPTY(Z)
    T = .T.
    ? "T = .T."
    ? EMPTY(T)
*   . . .
```

The User-Defined Function:

```
FUNCTION EMPTY
*
*  Program...: EMPTY
*  Author....: Phil Steele - President
*             Phillipps Computer Systems Inc.
*  Address...: 52 Hook Mountain Road,
*             Montville NJ 07045
*  Phone.....: (201) 575-8575
*  Date......: 01/02/89
*  Notice....: Copyright 1989  Philip Steele,
*             All Rights Reserved.
*  Notes.....: This function returns a .T. if a data
*             entry field contains blanks or a null.
*  Parameters: Passed - The variable to check for a
*                       blank or a null.
*
PARAMETERS Passed
PRIVATE     Z
Y = 0
Z = TYPE("Passed")
DO CASE
   CASE Z = "C" .OR. Z = "M"
      Y = LEN(ALLTRIM(Passed))
   CASE Z = "N" .OR. Z = "F"
      Y = Passed
   CASE Z = "D"
      Y = MONTH(Passed)
   CASE Z = "L"
      RETURN(Passed)
ENDCASE
RETURN IIF(Y=0, .T., .F.)
*END:EMPTY
```

Comments:

This User-Defined Function uses another UDF (ALLTRIM) to remove spaces from strings. It then checks for: a blank or null string for a string or memo field; a zero for any type of number; a month of zero for a date; and a logical FALSE for a logical. It returns TRUE or FALSE depending on the result.

LAST STRING OCCURRENCE

The problem:

You need to know the position of the LAST occurrence of string one in string two.

The solution:

Develop a User-Defined Function that finds the last location of string one in string two.

The calling code:

```
*   . . .
    SET COLOR TO &ColStand
    CLEAR
    X  =  "i"
    Y  =  "This is a test of the RAT function"
    Z  =  RAT(X,Y)
    ?  Z  && The last "i" is in position 32
*   . . .
```

The User-Defined Function:

```
FUNCTION RAT
*
* | Program...: RAT
* | Author....: Phil Steele - President
* |            Phillipps Computer Systems Inc.
* | Address...: 52 Hook Mountain Road,
* |            Montville NJ 07045
* | Phone.....: (201) 575-8575
* | Date......: 01/02/89
* | Notice....: Copyright 1989  Philip Steele,
* |            All Rights Reserved.
* | Notes.....: This procedure returns the location of
* |            the last occurrence of string1 in
* |            string2.
* | Parameters: Str1 - The string to look for.
* |            Str2 - The string to look at.
*
PARAMETERS Str1, Str2
PRIVATE Loc, Ans
Loc = 1
Ans = 0
DO WHILE Loc <> 0
   Loc  = AT(Str1, Str2)
   Ans  = IIF(Loc<>0, Loc+Ans, Ans)
   Str2 = SUBSTR(Str2,Loc+1)
ENDDO
RETURN(Ans)
*END:RAT
```

Comments:

This User-Defined Function uses a DO WHILE loop, and the dBASE IV internal function AT, to find the last occurrence of string one in string two.

KEY CODES

The problem:

> You need to know the code for various keys to use in a CHR(n) statement, and you do not have your dBASE IV manual handy.

The solution:

> Develop a User-Defined Function that returns the code needed.

The calling code:

```
*    . . .
     SET COLOR TO &ColStand
     CLEAR
     @22,13 SAY "Press any key to see its INKEY( ) "  =  ;
          "value – Esc to quit."
     A  =  FindKey
*    . . .
```

The User-Defined Function:

```
FUNCTION FINDKEY
*
*   Program...: FINDKEY
*   Author....: Phil Steele - President
*              Phillipps Computer Systems Inc.
*   Address...: 52 Hook Mountain Road,
*              Montville NJ 07045
*   Phone.....: (201) 575-8575
*   Date......: 01/02/89
*   Notice....: Copyright 1989  Philip Steele,
*              All Rights Reserved.
*   Notes.....: This function displays the dBASE IV
*              INKEY() value for the pressed key.
*   Parameters: None.
*   Note:.....: Press the Escape key to exit.
*
ViewChoice = 0
DO WHILE ViewChoice <> 27
   ViewChoice = INKEY()
   IF ViewChoice <> 0
      @12,61 SAY "     "
      @12,18 SAY "THE CONTROL CODE OF THE KEY " +;
                 "YOU PRESSED IS "
      @12,61 SAY ViewChoice PICTURE "9999"
   ENDIF
ENDDO
RETURN(.T.)
*END:FINDKEY
```

Comments:

This User-Defined Function displays the code returned by the dBASE IV internal function INKEY( ).

DOS ACCESS

The problem:

Your client wants to be able to access DOS, as well as perform some DOS functions from within your system.

The solution:

Develop a Procedure to access DOS and perform DOS functions.

The calling code:

```
*    . . .
     SET COLOR TO &ColStand
     CLEAR
     DO DoDOS
     SET COLOR TO &ColStand
     CLEAR
*    . . .
```

The Procedure:

```
PROCEDURE DODOS
*
* ┌─────────────────────────────────────────────────────────┐
* │ Program...: DODOS                                         │
* │ Author....: Phil Steele - President                       │
* │            Phillipps Computer Systems Inc.                │
* │ Address...: 52 Hook Mountain Road,                        │
* │            Montville NJ 07045                             │
* │ Phone.....: (201) 575-8575                                │
* │ Date......: 01/02/89                                      │
* │ Notice....: Copyright 1989  Philip Steele,                │
* │            All Rights Reserved.                           │
* │ Notes.....: This function returns the number of           │
* │            times string one is found in string            │
* │            two.                                           │
* │ Parameters: Str1 - The string to look for.                │
* │            Str2 - The string to look at to find           │
* │                   Str1.                                   │
* └─────────────────────────────────────────────────────────┘
DO SetUp

* * *   SECTION ONE - MENU * * *
DEFINE MENU DOS
DEFINE PAD UDOS OF DOS PROMPT;
     "1. Use DOS  " AT  9,33 MESSAGE;
     "Access DOS - Type EXIT to Return."
DEFINE PAD Cpy  OF DOS PROMPT;
     "2. Copy File " AT 10,33 MESSAGE;
     "Copy one file to another."
DEFINE PAD Dsk  OF DOS PROMPT;
     "3. Disk Copy " AT 11,33 MESSAGE;
     "Copy a diskette on A: to diskette on B:'
```

```
DEFINE PAD FmtA OF DOS PROMPT;
     "4. Format A: " AT 12,33 MESSAGE;
     "Format a disk on drive A: " +;
     "(1.2M on ATs - 1.4M on PS2s)"
DEFINE PAD FmtB OF DOS PROMPT;
     "5. Format B: " AT 13,33 MESSAGE;
     "Format a disk on drive B: (360K)"
DEFINE PAD Dir  OF DOS PROMPT;
     "6. Directory " AT 14,33 MESSAGE;
     "View the directory on the screen."
DEFINE PAD PDir OF DOS PROMPT;
     "7. Print Dir " AT 15,33 MESSAGE;
     "Print a listing of the directory."
DEFINE PAD BUp  OF DOS PROMPT;
     "8. Backup    " AT 16,33 MESSAGE;
     "Backup the databases and index files."
DEFINE PAD Res  OF DOS PROMPT;
     "9. Restore   " AT 17,33 MESSAGE;
     "Restore previous backed up " +;
     "databases and index files."
DEFINE PAD Ret  OF DOS PROMPT;
     "0. Return    " AT 18,33 MESSAGE;
     "Return to the Main Menu."
ON SELECTION PAD UDOS OF DOS DO DChoice WITH 1
ON SELECTION PAD Cpy  OF DOS DO DChoice WITH 2
ON SELECTION PAD Dsk  OF DOS DO DChoice WITH 3
ON SELECTION PAD FmtA OF DOS DO DChoice WITH 4
ON SELECTION PAD FmtB OF DOS DO DChoice WITH 5
ON SELECTION PAD Dir  OF DOS DO DChoice WITH 6
ON SELECTION PAD PDir OF DOS DO DChoice WITH 7
ON SELECTION PAD BUp  OF DOS DO DChoice WITH 8
ON SELECTION PAD Res  OF DOS DO DChoice WITH 9
ON SELECTION PAD Ret  OF DOS DO DChoice WITH 10
ACTIVATE MENU DOS
RETURN
*END:DODOS
* * * SECTION TWO - MENU ACTION * * *
* ─────────────────
PROCEDURE DCHOICE
* ─────────────────
PARAMETERS DOSChoice
PRIVATE    DOSChoice
SET COLOR TO &ColStand
CLEAR
DO CASE
* * * SECTION TWO - USE DOS * * *
   CASE DOSChoice = 1              && Use DOS
      RUN CD >TEMP.TXT
      SELECT J
      USE WhereAmI

* * * N O T E * * * N O T E * * * N O T E * * *
*                                             *
*     WhereAmI is a file                      *
*     consisting of one 240 character field   *
*     called DRIVE                            *
* * * N O T E * * * N O T E * * * N O T E * * *

      ZAP
      PACK
      APPEND FROM TEMP.TXT SDF
      Drv = SUBSTR(Drive,1,2)
```

```
            SDir = TRIM(SUBSTR(Drive,3))
            SAVE TO TEMP
            SET COLOR TO &ColStand
            CLEAR
            @ 0,0 SAY "Type EXIT to return to System"
            RUN COMMAND
            RUN &Drv>NUL
            RUN CD &SDir>NUL
            RESTORE FROM TEMP ADDITIVE
            RUN DEL TEMP.*>NUL
            SELECT A
* * * SECTION TWO - COPY FILE * * *
      CASE DOSChoice = 2                  && Copy File
            FromFile = "C:\FROMFILE.EXT            "
            ToFile   = "C:\TOFILE.EXT             "
            SET ESCAPE ON
            DO NoWinBox WITH 8,16,13,63,"D",.T.,"&ColHelp"
            @  9,17 SAY "Enter the name " +;
                        "of the file to be copied from"
            @ 11,17 SAY "Enter the name " +;
                        "of the file to be copied to"
            @ 10,25 GET FromFile  PICTURE "@!"
            @ 12,25 GET ToFile    PICTURE "@!"
            READ

            SET COLOR TO &ColStand
            SET ESCAPE OFF
            IF LASTKEY() <> Escape
               RUN COPY &FromFile &ToFile>NUL
            ENDIF
* * * SECTION TWO - DISK COPY A TO B * * *
      CASE DOSChoice = 3                  && DISKCOPY A to B
            SET COLOR TO &ColStand
            RUN DISKCOPY A: B:
* * * SECTION TWO - FORMAT A * * *
      CASE DOSChoice = 4                  && FORMAT A
            SET COLOR TO &ColStand
            RUN FORMAT A: /V
* * * SECTION TWO - FORMAT B * * *
      CASE DOSChoice = 5                  && FORMAT B
            SET COLOR TO &ColStand
            RUN FORMAT B: /V
* * * SECTION TWO - DISPLAY DIRECTORY * * *
      CASE DOSChoice = 6                  && DIRECTORY
            SET COLOR TO &ColStand
            RUN DIR/P
            WAIT
* * * SECTION TWO - PRINT DIRECTORY * * *
      CASE DOSChoice = 7                  && Print DIRECTORY
            DO NoWinBox WITH;
               10,19,14,60,"D",.T.,"&ColWarning"
            @ 11,21 SAY "Please make sure " +;
                        "the printer is ready."
            @ 13,25 SAY "Press Enter to start printing."
            Key = INKEY(0)
            @ 11,20 CLEAR TO 13,59
            @ 12,28 SAY "Printing the Directory."
            RUN DIR>LPT1
            SET DEVICE TO PRINT
            EJECT
            SET DEVICE TO SCREEN
* * * SECTION TWO - BACKUP DATA * * *
      CASE DOSChoice = 8                  && BACKUP
```

```
                    DO NoWinBox WITH 11,5,14,74,"S",.T.,"&ColHelp"
                    @ 12,9 SAY "Please Insert a Formatted " +;
                            "Diskette into Drive A: for the files."
                    @ 23,0 SAY ""
                    WAIT
                    @ 13,25 SAY "Backing Up the Database Files"
                    SET COLOR TO &ColStand
                    RUN COPY *.DBF A:>NUL
                    RUN COPY *.NTX A:>NUL
* * * SECTION TWO - RESTORE DATA * * *
    CASE DOSChoice = 9                     && RESTORE
                    DO NoWinBox WITH 11,5,14,74,"S",.T.,"&ColHelp"
                    @ 12,9 SAY "Please Insert the Diskette " +;
                            "with the Backed Up files in drive A."
                    @ 23,0 SAY ""
                    WAIT
                    @ 13,25 SAY "Restoring the Database Files"
                    SET COLOR TO &ColStand
                    RUN COPY A:*.DBF>NUL
                    RUN COPY A:*.NTX>NUL
* * * SECTION TWO - RETURN * * *
    CASE DOSChoice = 10                     && RETURN
                    DO AllDone
ENDCASE
DO SetUp
RETURN
*END:DCHOICE


* * * SECTION THREE - SETUP * * *
* ─────────────
PROCEDURE SETUP
* ─────────────
SET COLOR TO &ColStand
CLEAR
SET COLOR TO X
@ 7,33 CLEAR TO 20,50
SET COLOR TO &ColMenu
@ 6,32 CLEAR TO 19,48
@ 6,32        TO 19,48
@ 8,32        TO  8,48 DOUBLE
@ 8,32 SAY "╠"
@ 8,48 SAY "╣"
@ 7,37 SAY "D.O.S."
RETURN
*END:SETUP


* * * SECTION FOUR - ALL DONE * * *
* ─────────────
PROCEDURE ALLDONE
* ─────────────
DEACTIVATE MENU
RELEASE    MENU
SET COLOR TO &ColStand
RETURN TO MASTER
*END:ALLDONE
```

Comments:

This User-Defined Function is long, so we will examine it in sections:

Section 0—The *main procedure* DODOS first calls Setup.

Section 3 *Setup*—Clears the screen, draws a box for the menu and sets the colors to ColMenu (Yellow on Red).

Section 1 *Menu*—Defines the Menu "DOS" consisting of 10 choices. All 10 choices call the same procedure (DChoice).

Section 2 *Menu Action*—I use the typical method of implementing a menu: a DO CASE structure. This permits all the menu choices to be accommodated in one place.

Section 2 *Use DOS*—This is one of the tricky portions of the code. You must be able to return to the proper drive and directory after returning from the general DOS function. First, issue the DOS "CD >TEMP.TXT" command. This normally displays the current drive and sub-directory. However, by adding the ">" you redirect the output of the command to the "TEMP.TXT" file. Next, use a file called "WhereAmI" which you already defined. You could have created it here using the Procedure MAKEF. You ZAP this file and append the results of the TEMP.TXT file, which is an SDF file (System Data Format ASCII file). Then the drive letter and sub-directory are extracted. You save all the memory variables to the"TEMP" memory file, tell the user how to return to our system, and invoke a secondary command processor by using the "RUN COMMAND" command. Note, you must have enough memory available to use this option. After the user enters"EXIT" the code resumes where it left off. First, you change the default drive to the one you were in before COMMAND was run. The statement: "RUN &Drv>NUL" accomplishes this. In a like manner, the statement: "RUN CD &SDir>NUL" changes the subdirectory to the one you were in before running COMMAND. Now, all you have to do is restore the memory variables, delete the temporary file, and access the file you were in.

Section 2 *Copy file*—Place a box on the screen and prompt for the names of the files from and to which you are copying. If the escape key was not pressed, run the DOS COPY command.

Section 2 *Disk Copy A to B*—Run the DOS DISKCOPY command.

Section 2 *Format A*—Run the DOS FORMAT A: command with the /V (Volume label) option.

Section 2 *Format B*—Run the DOS FORMAT B: command with the /V (Volume label) option.

Section 2 *Display directory*—Run the DOS DIR command with the /P (Pause) option.

Section 2 *Print directory*—Run the DOS DIR command and redirect the output to the printer.

Section 2 *Backup data*—Place a box on the screen and instruct the user to insert a formatted diskette into drive A, then copy the databases and index files to the diskette.

Section 2 *Restore data*—Place a box on the screen, and instruct the user to insert a diskette with the files to be restored into drive A. Then, copy the databases and index files from the diskette.

Section 4 *All done*—Deactivate and release the DOS menu, reset the colors, and return to the Main procedure in the system "RETURN TO MASTER"

Index

Other Bestsellers From TAB

☐ **INCREASING PRODUCTIVITY WITH PFS® AND THE IBM® ASSISTANT SERIES—2ND EDITION—Burton**

If you use any or all of the popular PFS software modules . . . if you're thinking of investing in this highly versatile business tool . . . or if you're interested in discovering an exclusive source for practical, problem-solving "templates" to help you access maximum productivity power from each and ever PFS module . . . You can't afford to miss this completely revised, updated, and expanded new second edition of *Increasing Productivity with PFS and the IBM Assistant Series*! 256 pp., 240 illus., 7″ × 10″.
Paper $21.95   **Hard $22.95**
Book No. 2729

☐ **PROGRAMMING WITH dBASE III® PLUS—Prague and Hammitt**

Packed with expert programming techniques and shortcuts, this is an essential guide to Ashton Tate's newest version of it dBASE relational database manager for the IBM® PC™. It includes all the practical, use-it-now advice and guidance beginning PC users are looking for . . . as well as power programming techniques that will allow more advanced users to increase productivity while sharply reducing application development time. 384 pp., 150 illus., 7″ × 10″.
Paper $21.95   **Hard $29.95**
Book No. 2726

☐ **SUPERCALC® 3: LEARNING, USING AND MASTERING—Willis and Pasewark**

Whether you're a first-time spreadsheet user who wants a thorough introduction to SuperCalc 3 . . . a SuperCalc user who is upgrading to Version 3 . . . or an experienced business programmer who is switching from another spreadsheet program . . . you will find this an essential guide to mastering all the powerful, updated, multifaceted features offered by this amazing business tool! In no time at all you'll be putting your IBM® PC, PCjr, Apple® IIe, or TI Professional to work in dozens of number-crunching ways using SuperCalc 3—the powerful electronic spreadsheet that lets you custom design your own microcomputer program for organizing, arranging, and manipulating all types of information. 256 pp., 125 illus., 7″ × 10″.
Paper $16.95   **Hard $22.95**
Book No. 2694

☐ **HARVARD PROJECT MANAGER/TOTAL PROJECT MANAGER: CONTROLLING YOUR RESOURCES—Kasevich**

Whether involved in engineering, manufacturing, publishing, agriculture, retailing, or government, today's "smart" managers are discovering that a desk-top or personal computer and the right software are essential ingredients for success. And nowhere is this more important than in project management—the defining and organizing of all aspects of a project so that time and resources can be put to most productive use. 240 pp., 180 illus., 7″ × 10″.
Paper $16.95   **Hard $21.95**
Book No. 2678

☐ **MULTIMATE® USER'S GUIDE—Spear and Ritchie**

Unlike the user's manuals that come with MultiMate or other books that simply restate what's already in those user's manuals, *MultiMate® User's Guide* provides a wealth of "inside" information on MultiMate's special utilities and shows you how to create a wide range of business documents successfully. Authors Barbara Spead and Deborah Ritchie also include handy "from experience" tips and hints that eliminate the frustration of trying to figure out MultiMate's more elusive applications potential and makes it possible for you to write professional-quality documents right from the start. 192 pp., 7″ × 10″.
Paper $14.95   **Hard $21.95**
Book No. 2623

☐ **WORKING WITH DISPLAYWRITE 3—Krumm**

At last, a thorough, hands-on guide that shows you how to make documents that look exactly as you want them to . . . precise, professional, attractive, and eye-catching. This first, easy-to-follow handbook on mastering IBM's state-of-the-art word-processing program, DisplayWrite 3, will help you present an image of your company or business that clearly demands respect. 320 pp., 7″ × 10″.
Paper $17.95   **Hard $24.95**
Book No. 2664

Other Bestsellers From TAB

☐ **ADVANCED dBASE III® APPLICATIONS—Baker**

An invaluable collection of ready-to-use dBASE III applications for getting maximum productivity from Ashton Tate's state-of-the-art database management software! Includes how-to's for setting up and maintaining computerized files for managing employees, payroll, inventory, accounting applications, time management, tracking sales and performing marketing research, and more. 448 pp., 120 illus., 7″ × 10″.

Paper $21.95 **Hard $28.95**
Book No. 2618

☐ **PROGRAMMING WITH dBASE III®**

With this excellent sourcebook at your side, using dBASE III is a snap! You'll discover how to take advantage of all this fourth generation software's data handling capabilities *plus* learn how to unlock the power of dBASE III as a complete programming language! Also includes an appendix detailing the differences between dBASE II and dBASE III, with full instructions for using dConvert—the utility program used to convert dBASE II programs to dBASE III! 304 pp., 215 illus., 7″ × 10″.

Paper $17.95 **Book No. 1976**

☐ **MASTERING SYMPHONY™—Bolocan**

Anyone who's purchased the new Symphony package from Lotus . . . or who's thinking of trading up from Lotus 1-2-3™ . . . will find this an essential guide! Covering each of Symphony's functions separately and in-depth, this unique guide clarifies and gives sample programs and diagrams to demonstrate the software's spreadsheet, work processing, data management, graphics, and communications features. 240 pp., 170 illus., 7″ × 10″.

Paper $16.95 **Hard $22.95**
Book No. 1948

☐ **FRAMEWORK™ APPLICATIONS—Baker**

A hands-on overview of Ashton Tate's state-of-the-art Framework™—including a collection of practical, ready-to-use applications that can be used to solve a variety of real-world problems! You'll use all of the components of the Framework integrated package including spreadsheet, database, word processing, programming language, even how to design your own original programs using Framework as a base. 272 pp., 178 illus., 7″ × 10″.

Paper $16.95 **Hard $26.95**
Book No. 1908

☐ **ADVANCED SYMPHONY™ APPLICATIONS— Bolocan**

Now software expert David Bolocan takes you beyond the beginner's tutorial and shows you how to successfully channel Symphony's data crunching powers for everything from analyzing stock investments to managing your taxes. No matter what your needs—home use, small business management, or corporate administration—this hands-on guide will help you orchestrate it all. 240 pp., 190 illus., 7″ × 10″.

Paper $16.95 **Hard $23.95**
Book No. 1988

☐ **MONEY MANAGEMENT WORKSHEETS FOR 1-2-3™/SYMPHONY™—Maffin**

Turn your IBM PC® or PC-compatible into a full-time financial manager with the help of this huge collection of over 60 customized worksheets designed especially for the powerful 1-2-3/Symphony business software! Using these invaluable worksheets,you can do everything from balancing your checkbook and planning your budget to managing investments, even playing the stock market. 192 pp., 30 illus., 7″ × 10″.

Paper $14.95 **Hard $21.95**
Book No. 1968

☐ **HOW TO RUN YOUR BUSINESS WITH dBASE II®—Baker**

With this book at your side, you can set up personnel records, perform payroll duties, keep inventory, pay bills, and more. You can actually incorporate big business management techniques into your small business, easily and profitably. Everything you need to run your business with dBASE is included . . . what dBASE II can do and how you can get professional results. 320 pp., 144 illus., 7″ × 10″.

Paper $16.95 **Hard $26.95**
Book No. 1918

☐ **dBASE II®—A COMPREHENSIVE USER'S MANUAL—Bharucha**

A logical, easy-to-follow guide that takes you from computer novice to expert programmer in dBASE II! Just some of the unique features that set this guide apart from ordinary user manuals include: How to create and maintain a database: Explanations of dBASE functions: Details on how to use COPY to create standard text files from dBASE files . . . a requirement for communicating with other software; and much more. 320 pp., 7″ × 10″.

Paper $18.95 **Hard $24.95**
Book No. 1884

Other Bestsellers From TAB

85 dBASE IV
User-Defined Functions and Procedures

If you are intrigued with the possibilities of the programs included in *85 dBASE IV User-Defined Functions and Procedures* (TAB Book No. 3236), you definitely should consider having the ready-to-run disk containing the software applications. This software is guaranteed free of manufacturer's defects. (If you have any problems, return the disk within 30 days, and we'll send you a new one.) Interested?

Available on a 5.25-inch, PC-DOS 9 sector double-sided diskette for IBM PC/XT/AT and compatible computers. Price is $49.95, $1.50 plus shipping and handling.